Jeanie Thomas Gould Lincoln

An Unwilling Maid

Being the History of Certain Episodes During the American Revolution

Jeanie Thomas Gould Lincoln

An Unwilling Maid
Being the History of Certain Episodes During the American Revolution

ISBN/EAN: 9783744704908

Printed in Europe, USA, Canada, Australia, Japan

Cover: Foto ©Thomas Meinert / pixelio.de

More available books at **www.hansebooks.com**

BETTY WOLCOTT

An
Unwilling Maid

Being the History of Certain Episodes during the American Revolution in the Early Life of Mistress Betty Yorke, born Wolcott

By JEANIE GOULD LINCOLN

"O Romeo, Romeo! wherefore art thou Romeo?"

BOSTON AND NEW YORK
HOUGHTON, MIFFLIN AND COMPANY
The Riverside Press, Cambridge
1897

TO A NINETEENTH CENTURY GIRL.

A great-grandmother's bewitching face,
　　Looks forth from this olden story,
For Love is a master who laughs at place,
　　And scoffs at both Whig and Tory.

To-day if he comes, as a conqueror may,
　　To a heart untouched by his flame,
Be loyal as she of the olden day,
　　That Eighteenth Century dame !

CONTENTS

LIST OF ILLUSTRATIONS

AN UNWILLING MAID

CHAPTER I

MISS MOPPET

It was a warm summer day. Not too
warm, for away up in the Connecticut hills
the sun seemed to temper its rays, and down
among the shadows of the trees surrounding
Great Pond there were cool, shady glades
where one could almost fancy it was May
instead of hot July.

At a point not far from the water, leaning against the trunk of a stately maple,
stood a young man. His head, from which
he had raised a somewhat old and weather-
beaten hat, was finely formed, and covered
with chestnut curls; his clothes, also shabby
and worn, were homespun and ill-fitting,
but his erect military carriage, with an in-
describable air of polish and fine breeding,
seemed strangely incongruous in connection

with his apparel and travel-worn appearance.

"I wonder where I am," he said half
aloud, as he surveyed the pretty sheet of
water sparkling in the afternoon sun.
"Faith, 't is hard enough to be half starved
and foot-sore, without being lost in an enemy's country. The woman who gave me that
glass of milk at five o'clock this morning
said I was within a mile of Goshen. I must
have walked ten miles since then, and am
apparently no nearer the line than I was
yesterday — Hark! what 's that?" — as a
sound of voices struck his ear faintly, coming from some distance on his right. "Some
one comes in this direction. I had best conceal myself in these friendly bushes until I
ascertain whether 't is friend or foe."

So saying, he plunged hastily into a
thicket of low-lying shrubs close at hand,
and, throwing himself flat upon the ground
under them, was comparatively secure from
observation as long as he remained perfectly
still. The next sound he heard was horses'
feet, moving at a walk, and presently there
came in view a spirited-looking bay mare
and a gray pony, the riders being engaged
in merry conversation.

"No, no, Betty," said the little girl of
about nine years, who rode the pony; "it is
just here, or a few rods farther on, where we
had the Maypole set last year, and I know
I can find the herbs which Chloe wants
near by on the shore of the pond. Let's
dismount and tie the horses here, and you
and I can search for them."

"It's well I did not let you come alone,"
said the rider of the bay mare, laughing as
she spoke. "Truly, Miss Moppet, you are
a courageous little maid to wish to venture
in these woods. Not that I am afraid,"
said Betty Wolcott suddenly, remembering
the weight and dignity of her sixteen years
as compared with her little sister, "but
in these troublous times father says it were
well to be careful."

"Since when have you grown so staid?"
said Miss Moppet, shaking her long yellow
hair back from her shoulders as she jumped
off her pony and led him up to a young ash-
tree, whose branches allowed of her securing
him by the bridle to one of them. "Of all
people in the world, Betty, you to read me a
lecture on care-taking," and with a mischievous laugh the child fled around the tree in
pretended dismay, as Betty sprang to the

ground and shook her riding-whip playfully in her direction.

"Ungrateful Moppet," she said, as she tied both horses to the tree beside her, "did I not rescue you from punishment for dire naughtiness in the pantry and beg Aunt Euphemia to pardon you, and then go for the horses, which Reuben was too busy to saddle.

"Yes, my own dear Betty," cried the small sinner, emerging suddenly from the friendly shelter and seizing her round the waist, "but you know this soberness is but 'skin-deep,' as Chloe says, and you need not cease to be merry because you are sixteen since yesterday. Come, let's find the herbs," and joining hands the two ran swiftly off to the shore, Betty tucking up her habit with easy grace as she went. The occupant of the covert raised his head carefully and looked after the pair, the sound of their voices growing faint as they pushed their way through the undergrowth which intercepted their progress.

"What a lovely creature!" he ejaculated, raising himself on one elbow. "I wonder who she is, and how she comes in this wild neighborhood. Perhaps I am not so very

far off my road after all; they must have
come from a not very distant home, for the
horses are not even wet this warm day.
Egad, that mare looks as if she had plenty
of speed in her; 't would not be a bad idea
to throw my leg over her back and be off,
and so distance those who even now may be
pursuing me." He half rose as the thought
occurred to him, but in an instant sank
back under the leaves.

"How would her mistress fare without
her?" he said ruefully "'Tis not to be
thought of; they may be miles from home,
even here, and I am too much a squire of
dames to take such unkind advantage.
There must be some other way out of my
present dilemma than this," and rolling over
on the mixture of grass and dry leaves which
formed his resting-place he lay still and
began to ponder.

Half an hour passed; the shadows began
to deepen as the sun crept down in the sky,
and the horses whinnied at each other as if
to remind their absent riders that supper-
time was approaching. But the girls did
not return, and the thoughts which occupied
the young wanderer were so engrossing that
he did not hear a cry which began faintly

and then rose to a shriek agonized enough
to pierce his reverie.

" Good heavens!" he cried, springing to
his feet, as borne on the summer wind the
frantic supplication came to him —

" Help, help! oh, will nobody come!"
and then the sobbing cry again — " help!"

The tall muscular form straightened itself
and sped through the bushes, crushing them
down on either side with a strong arm, as he
went rapidly in the direction of the cries.

" Courage! I am coming," he cried, as,
gaining the shore of the pond, he saw what
had happened. Just beyond his halting-
place there was a jutting bank, and over-
hanging it a large tree, whose branches
almost touched the water beneath. At the
top of the bank stood the elder of the two
girls; she had torn off the skirt of her rid-
ing-habit, and was about to leap down into
the water where a mass of floating yellow
hair and a wisp of white gown told their
story of disaster. As he ran the stranger
flung off his coat, but there was no time to
divest himself of his heavy riding-boots, so
in he plunged and struck out boldly with
the air of a strong and competent swimmer.

The pond, like many of our small inland

lakes, was shallow for some distance from the shore, and then suddenly shelved in unexpected quarters, developing deep holes where the water was so cold that its effect on a swimmer was almost dangerous. Into one of these depths the little girl had evidently plunged, and realizing the cause of her sudden disappearance the stranger dived with great rapidity at the spot where the golden hair had gone down. His first attempt failed; but as the child partially rose for the second time, he caught the little figure and with skillful hand supported her against his shoulder, as he struck out for the shore, which he reached quickly, but chilled almost to the bone from the coldness of the water.

"Do not be so alarmed," he said, as Betty, with pallid cheeks and trembling hands, knelt beside the unconscious child on the grass; "she will revive; her heart beats and she is not very cold. Let me find my coat," and he stumbled as he rose to go in search of it.

"It is here," gasped Betty; "I fetched it on my way down the slope; oh, sir, do you think she lives?"

For answer the young man produced from

an inner pocket of his shabby garment a
small flask, which he uncorked and held
toward her.

"It is cognac," he said; "put a drop or
two between her lips while I chafe her
hands, — so; see, she revives," as the white
lids quivered for a second, and then the
pretty blue eyes opened.

"Moppet, Moppet, my darling," cried her
sister, "are you hurt? Did you strike anything in your fall?"

"Why, Betty!" ejaculated the child,
"why are you giving me nasty stuff; here
are the tansy leaves," and she held up her
left hand, where tightly clenched she had
kept the herbs, whose gathering on the edge
of the treacherous bank had been her undoing.

"You are a brave little maid," said the
stranger, as he put the flask to his own lips.
"The shock will be all you have to guard
against, and even that is passing;" for Miss
Moppet had staggered upon her feet and
was looking with astonished eyes at her
dripping clothing.

"Did I fall, Betty?" she said. "Why
my gown is sopping wet, — oh! have I been
at the bottom of the pond?"

" You had stopped there, sweetheart, but for this good gentleman," said Betty, holding out a small, trembling hand to the stranger, a lovely smile dimpling her cheeks as she spoke. " Sir, with all my heart I thank you. My little sister had drowned but for your promptness and skill ; I do not know how to express my gratitude."

" I am more than rewarded for my simple service," replied the young man, raising the pretty hand to his lips with a profound bow and easy grace, " but I am afraid your sister may get a chill, as the sun is so low in the sky ; and if I may venture upon a suggestion, it would be well to ride speedily to some shelter where she can obtain dry clothing. If you will permit me to offer you the cape of my riding-coat (which is near at hand) I will wrap her in it at once, and then I think she will be safe from any after-effects of her cold bath in the pond."

" Oh, you are too kind," cried Betty, as the stranger disappeared in the underbrush. " Moppet, Moppet, what can we say to prove our gratitude ? You had been drowned twice over but for him."

" Ask him to come to the manor," said Miss Moppet, much less agitated than her sister, and being always a small person of many resources. "Father will be glad to bid him welcome, and you know " —

"Yes," interrupted Betty, as their new friend appeared at her elbow with a cape of dark blue cloth over his arm.

" Here is my cape," he said, " and though not very large it will cover her sufficiently. Let me untie your horses and help you to mount."

" Oh, we can mount alone," said Miss Moppet, who had by this time recovered her spirits, " but you must come home with us; you are dripping wet yourself; and if you like, you may ride my pony. He has carried double before now, and I am but a light weight, as my father says."

" Will you not come home with us?" asked Betty wistfully. " My father, General Wolcott, is away just now from the manor, but he will have warm welcome and hearty thanks, believe me, for the strength and courage which have rescued his youngest child from yonder grave," and Betty shuddered and grew pale again at the very thought of what Miss Moppet had escaped.

" General Wolcott," said the stranger, with a start. " Ah, then you are his daughters. And he is away?"

"Yes," said Betty, as they walked toward the tree where the horses were tied. "There has been a raid upon our coast by Governor Tryon and his Hessians; we got news three days ago of the movement of the Loyalists, and my father, with my brother Oliver, has gone to the aid of the poor people at Fairfield. Do you know of it, sir? Have you met any of our troops?"

"I have seen them," said the stranger briefly, with a half smile curving his handsome mouth, "but they are not near this point"—and beneath his breath he added, "I devoutly hope not."

"Which way are you traveling?" asked Betty, as she stood beside her bay mare. "Surely you will not refuse to come to the manor? Aunt Euphemia and my elder sister are there, and we will give you warm welcome."

"I thank you," said the stranger, with great courtesy, "but I must be on my way westward before night overtakes me. Can you tell me how many miles I am from Goshen, which I left this morning?"

"You are within Litchfield township," said Betty. "We are some four miles from my father's house. Pray, sir, come

with us; I fear for your health from that
sudden plunge into the icy waters of our
pond."

"Oh, no," said the stranger, laughing. "I
were less than man to mind a bath of this
sort. With all my heart I thank you for
your solicitude; that I am unable to accept
your hospitality you must lay at the door of
circumstances which neither you nor I can
control."

"But your cape, sir," faltered Betty, her
eyes dropping, as she blushed under the
ardent yet respectful gaze which sought
hers; "how are we to return that? And
you may need it; I am sorely afraid you
will yet suffer for your kindness."

"Not I," said the stranger, pressing her
hand, as he gave the reins into her fingers;
"as for the cape, keep it until we meet
again, and — farewell!"

But Miss Moppet threw her arms around
his neck as he bent over the gray pony and
secured the cape more tightly around her
small shoulders.

"I have n't half thanked you," she said,
"but I will do so properly some day, when
you come to Wolcott Manor. Farewell,"
and waving her little hand in adieu, the

horses moved away, and were presently lost to sight in the underbrush.

" Egad! " said the stranger, gazing after them, as he picked up his coat and started for the spot where he had left his hat. " What a marvelous country it is! The soldiers are uncouth farmer lads, yet they fight and die like heroes, and the country maids have the speech and air of court ladies. Geoffrey Yorke, you have wandered far afield; I would you had time and chance to meet that lovely rebel again!" and with a deep-drawn sigh he plunged farther into the woods.

CHAPTER II

"Oh, Betty, Betty," cried Miss Moppet, as the pair gained the more frequented road and cantered briskly on their homeward way, "what an adventure we have had! Aunt Euphemia will no doubt bestow a sound rating on me, for, alas!"—with a doleful glance downward—"see the draggled condition of my habit."

"Never mind your habit, Moppet," said Betty. "Thank Heaven instead that you are not lying stiff and cold at the bottom of the pond. You can never know the agony I suffered when I saw you fall; I should have plunged in after you in another second."

"Dearest Betty," said the child, looking lovingly at her, "I know you can swim, but you never could have held me up as that stranger did. Oh!" with sudden recollection, "we did not ask his name! Did you forget?"

"No," said Betty, "but when I told him

ours and he did not give his name in return,
I thought perhaps he did not care to be
known, and of course forbore to press him."

"How handsome he was," said Moppet;
"did you see his hair? And how tightly it
curled, wet as it was? And his eyes —
surely you noted his eyes, Betty?"

"Yes," replied Betty, blushing with remembrance of the parting glance the hazel
eyes had bestowed upon her; "he is a personable fellow enough."

"Far handsomer than Josiah Huntington," said Moppet mischievously, "or even
Francis Plunkett."

"What does a little maid like you know
of looks?" said Betty reprovingly, "and
what would Aunt Euphemia say to such
comments, I wonder?"

"You'll never tell tales of me," said
Moppet, with the easy confidence of a
spoiled child. "Do you think he was a soldier — perhaps an officer from Fort Trumbull, like the one Oliver brought home last
April?"

"Very likely," said Betty. "Are you
cold, Moppet? I am so afraid you may
suffer; stop talking so fast and muffle yourself more closely in the cape. We must be

hastening home," and giving her horse the whip, they rode rapidly down hill.

Wolcott Manor, the home of which Betty spoke, was a fine, spacious house situated on top of the hills, where ran a broad plateau which later in its history developed into a long and broad street, on either side of which were erected dwellings which have since been interwoven with the stateliest names in old Connecticut. The house was double, built in the style of the day, with a hall running through it, and large rooms on either side, the kitchen, bakery, and well-house all at the back, and forming with the buttery a sort of L, near but not connecting with the different outhouses. It was shingled from top to bottom, and the dormer windows, with their quaint panes, rendered it both stately and picturesque. As the girls drew rein at the small porch, on the south side of the mansion, a tall, fine-looking woman of middle age, her gray gown tucked neatly up, and a snowy white apron tied around her shapely waist, appeared at the threshold of the door.

"Why, Betty," she said in a surprised voice, " you have been absent so long that I was about to send Reuben in search of you.

The boxes are undone, and we need your
help; Moppet — why, what ails the child?"
and Miss Euphemia Wolcott paused in dismay as she surveyed Miss Moppet's still
damp habit and disheveled hair.

"I've been at the very bottom of Great
Pond," announced the child, enjoying the
situation with true dramatic instinct, "and
Betty has all the herbs for Chloe safe in her
basket."

"What does the child mean?" asked her
bewildered aunt, unfastening the heavy cloth
cape from the small shoulders, and perceiv-
ing that she had had a thorough wetting.

"It is true, Aunt Euphemia," said Betty,
springing off her mare and throwing the
reins to Reuben as he came slowly around
the house. "We were on one of the hillocks
overlooking the pond, and somehow — it all
happened so swiftly that I cannot tell how
— but Moppet must have ventured too near
the edge, for the treacherous soil gave way,
and down she pitched into the water before
I could put out hand to stay her. I think I
screamed, and then I was pulling off my
habit-skirt to plunge after her when a young
man ran hastily along the shore below and
cried out to me, 'Courage!' and he threw

off his coat and dived down, down," — Betty
shuddered and turned pale, — "and then he
caught Moppet's skirt and held her up until
he swam safely to shore with her. She was
quite unconscious, but by chafing her hands
and giving her some spirits (which the
young stranger had in his flask) we recovered her, and, indeed, I think she is none
the worse for her experience," and Betty
put both arms around her little sister and
hugged her warmly, bursting into tears,
which until now had been so carefully restrained.

"Thank Heaven!" cried Miss Euphemia,
kissing them both. "You could never have
rescued her alone, Betty; perhaps you
might both have drowned. Where is the
brave young man who came to your aid? I
trust you gave him clear directions how to
reach the house."

"He would not come," answered Betty
simply; "he said he was traveling westward,
and I thought he seemed anxious to be off."

"But we pressed him, Aunt Euphemia,"
put in Moppet, "and I told him my pony
could carry double. And I do not know
how we will return his cape; do you?"

"You must come indoors at once and get

dry clothing," said her aunt, "and I will tell Chloe to make you a hot posset lest you get a chill; run quickly, Moppet, and do not stand a moment longer in those wet clothes. Now, Betty," as the child disappeared inside, "have you any idea who this stranger can be, or whence he came?"

"I have not," said Betty, blushing rosy red (though she could not have told why) under her aunt's close scrutiny.

"What did he look like?" questioned Miss Euphemia.

"Like a young man of spirit," said Betty, mischief getting the better of her, "and he had a soldierly air to boot and spoke with command."

"I trust with all due respect as well," said Miss Euphemia gravely.

"Truly, he both spoke and behaved as a gentleman should."

"Do you think it could be Oliver's friend, young Otis from Boston?" said Miss Euphemia. "He was to arrive in these parts this week."

"It may be he," said Betty, "ask Pamela, she has met him;" and as she turned to enter she almost fell into the arms of a tall, slender girl who was hurrying forth to meet her.

At first glance there was enough of likeness between the girls to say that they
might be sisters, but the next made the
resemblance less, and their dissimilarity of
expression and coloring increased with acquaintance. Both had the same slender,
graceful figure, but while Betty was of
medium height, Pamela was distinctly taller
than her sister, and her pretty head was
covered with golden hair, while Betty's lux-
uriant locks were that peculiar shade which
is neither auburn nor golden, but a combination of both, and her eyes were hazel-
gray, with long lashes much darker than her
hair. Both girls wore their hair piled on
top of the head, as was the fashion of the
time, and both were guiltless of powder, but
Pamela's rebellious waves were trained to
lie as close as she could make them, while
Betty's would crop out into little dainty
saucy curls over her forehead and down the
nape of her slender neck in a most bewilder-
ing fashion. Their complexions, like Miss
Moppet's, were exquisitely satin-like in tex-
ture, but there was no break in Pamela's
smooth cheeks, whereas Betty's dimples
lurked not only around her willful mouth,
but perched high in her right cheek, and you

found yourself unconsciously watching to
see them come and go at the tricksy maid's
changing will. There was but little more
than a year's difference in their ages, yet
Betty seemed almost a child beside Pamela's
gracious stateliness.

"What is it all about?" asked the bewildered Pamela, catching hold of Betty.
" Moppet dashes into the kitchen, damp and
moist, and says she has been at the bottom
of the pond, and orders hot posset, and you,
Betty, have an air of fright " —

"I should think she might well," interrupted Miss Euphemia : " I will tell you,
Pamela — Betty, go upstairs and change
your habit for a gown, and then come down
to assist me. We are about to mould the
bullets."

" Oh, Aunt Euphemia ! " cried Betty, interrupting in her turn, " I beg your pardon,
but did those huge boxes contain the leaden
statue of King George, as my father's letter
advised us ? "

" It was cut in pieces, Betty," said Pamela demurely.

" As if I did n't know that," flashed out
Betty ; " and that it disappeared after the
patriots hauled it down in Bowling Green,

and that General Washington recommended
it should be used for the cause of Freedom,
and that we are all to help transform it into
bullets for our soldiers, — truly, Pamela, I
have not forgot my father's account of it,"
and Betty vanished inside the door with a
rebellious toss of her head, resenting the im-
plied air of elder sister which Pamela sometimes indulged in.

"Our little Moppet has come perilously
near death," said Miss Euphemia, following
Pamela into the house. "She has been rescued from drowning in Great Pond by a
gentleman whom Betty had never seen before. She describes him as a fine personable
youth, and I think it may be Oliver's friend,
young Otis, who is expected at the Tracys'
on a visit from Boston."

"It can hardly be he, aunt," said Pamela,
"for Sally Tracy has just told me that he
will not arrive for two days, and moreover
he comes with Mrs. Foster and Patty War-
ren, who are glad to take him as escort in
these troublous times. I will run up to
Moppet, for the girls are waiting for you ;
the lead got somewhat overheated, and they
want your advice as to using it."

Miss Euphemia went slowly down the

hall and through the large dining-room, pausing as she passed to knock at a small door opening off the hall into a sitting-room.

" Are you there, Miss Bidwell ? " she said, as a small elderly woman, with bent figure and pleasant, shrewd face, rose from her chair in response. " Will you kindly go up and see that Miss Moppet be properly rubbed and made dry, and let her take her hot posset, and then, if not too tired, she may come to me in the kitchen."

Miss Bidwell, who was at once housekeeper, manager, and confidential servant to the Wolcott household, gave a cheerful affirmative ; and as she laid down the stocking she was carefully darning, and prepared to leave the room, Miss Euphemia resumed her interrupted walk toward the kitchen.

Standing and sitting around the great kitchen fireplace were a group of young people, whose voices rose in a lively chorus as she entered. Over the fire, on a crane, hung a large kettle, from the top of which issued sounds of spluttering and boiling, and a young man was in the act of endeavoring to lift it amid cries of remonstrance.

" Have a care, Francis," cried a pretty, roguish-looking girl in a gray homespun

gown, brandishing a wet towel as she spoke;
"hot lead will be your portion if you dare
trifle with that boiling pot. What are we to
do with it, Miss Euphemia?" as that lady
came forward in haste; "a few drops of
water flirted out of my towel and must have
fallen inside, for 't is spluttering in terrific
fashion."

"Shall I lift it off the fire?" asked the
young man, whose name was Francis Plunkett.

"Certainly," said Miss Euphemia, in-
specting the now tranquil kettle; "here are
the moulds all greased; gently, now," as
she put a small ladle inside the pot; "now
move it slowly, and put the pot here beside
me on the table."

"Will they really turn out bullets?"
asked another girl in a whisper, as Sally
Tracy moved a second big pot with the intention of hanging it on the fire, but was
prevented by a tall, silent young man, who
stopped his occupation of sorting out bits of
lead to assist her.

"Thank you, Josiah," said Sally. "Turn
out bullets, Dolly? — why, of course, when
they come out of the moulds. What did you
suppose we were all about?"

Dolly Trumbull (who was on a visit to the Wolcotts') looked shy and somewhat distressed, and promptly retired into a corner, where she resumed her conversation with her cousin, Josiah Huntington; and presently Betty came flying into the kitchen, her gown tucked up ready for work, and full of apologies for her tardy appearance. Sally Tracy, who was Betty's sworn friend and companion in all her fun and frolics, pounced upon her at once; but as Miss Euphemia called them both to assist her with the moulds, Betty had to reserve the story of her adventure until a more propitious moment.

"Has there been any news from Oliver since he set forth on this last expedition?" asked Dolly.

"It is too soon yet to hear," said Josiah, "though possibly by to-morrow some intelligence may reach us. Francis and I did not reach here from New Haven for four days, and we return there on Saturday. As it was, I left only in obedience to my father's command, and brought news of Lyon's ravaging the city to General Wolcott, dodging Hessians and outlying marauders by the way. Do you stop here long,

Dolly, or will you have my escort back to
Lebanon?"

"I came for a month," answered Dolly;
"I was ill of spring fever, and since then
my mother thinks this mountain air benefits
me. But you go back to your duties at Yale
College, though it's early yet for them."

"My students and I have spent our va-
cation handling cartridges," said Josiah
grimly, for he was a tutor at Yale, and had
done yeoman service in the defense of New
Haven. "'T is a sorry sight to see our
beautiful city now laid waste; but that our
faith is strong in the Continental Congress
and General Washington, I know not how
heart could bear it."

"Who speaks of faith?" said Pamela's
gentle voice, as she slipped into a chair on
Dolly's right. "I think hope is ever a better watchword."

"Aye," murmured Huntington, as Dolly
summoned courage to cross the room, "it is
one I will carry ever with me, Pamela, if *you*
bid me do so."

"I did not mean," faltered Pamela, casting down her dove-like eyes, but not so
quickly that she did not see the ardent
glance of her lover, "I — that is — oh yes,

Aunt Euphemia," with sudden change of tone, " it is growing somewhat dark, and we had better leave the moulds to harden. Shall I tell Miss Bidwell that you are ready for supper ? "

To which Miss Euphemia returned an affirmative, and the whole party trooped back to the dining-room, Pamela leading the way, and Huntington following her with a half-mischievous smile curving his usually grave mouth.

CHAPTER III

OLIVER'S PRISONER

"I don't care anything about it," said Miss Moppet with decision. "It's a nasty, horrid letter, and I've made it over and over, and it will not get one bit plainer. Count one, two, jump one; then two stitches plain; it's no use at all, Miss Bidwell, I cannot make it any better." And with a deep sigh Miss Moppet surveyed her sampler, where she had for six weeks been laboriously trying to inscribe "Faith Wolcott, her sampler, aged nine," with little success and much loss of temper.

"W is a hard letter," said Miss Bidwell, laying down one of the perpetual stockings with which she seemed always supplied for mending purposes; "you will have to rip this out again: the first stroke is too near the letter before it:" and she handed the unhappy sampler back to the child.

"It's always like that," said Miss Moppet

in a tone of exasperation. " I think a sampler is the very *devil!* "

" Oh," said Miss Bidwell in a shocked voice, " I shall have to report you as a naughty chit if you use such language."

" Well, it just *is*," said Moppet; " that 's what the minister said in his sermon Sunday week, and you know, Miss Bidwell, that you admired it extremely, because I heard you tell Pamela so."

" Admired the devil?" said Miss Bidwell. " Child, what are you talking about?"

" The sermon," said Miss Moppet, breaking her silk for the fourth time; " the minister said the devil went roaring up and down the earth seeking whom he might devour. Would n't I like to hear him roar. Do you conceive it is like a bull or a lion's roar?"

" The Bible says a lion," said Miss Bidwell, looking all the more severe because she was so amused.

" I am truly sorry for that poor devil," said Miss Moppet, heaving a deep sigh. " Just think how tired he must become, and how much work he must have to do. O—o—oh!" — a prolonged scream — " he certainly has possession of my sampler" —

dancing up and down with pain — "for that needle has gone one inch into my thumb!"

"Come here and let me bind it up," said Miss Bidwell, seizing the small sinner as she whirled past her. "How often must I tell you not to give way to such sinful temper? And talking about the devil is not proper for little girls."

"Why not just as well as for older folk?" said Moppet, submitting to have a soft bit of rag bound around the bleeding thumb. "I think the devil ought to be prayed for if he's such an abominable sinner — yes, I do." And Moppet, whose belief in a personal devil was evidently large, surveyed Miss Bidwell with uncompromising eyes.

"Tut!" said Miss Bidwell, to whom this novel idea savored of ungodliness, but wishing to be lenient toward the child whose adoring slave she was. "Miss Euphemia would be shocked to hear you."

"I shall not tell her," said the child shrewdly, "but I am going to pray for the devil each night, whether any one else does or not."

"As you cannot work any longer on the sampler, you had best go to Miss Pamela for your writing lesson," said Miss Bidwell.

" Pamela is out in the orchard with Josiah Huntington," said Moppet, " and she would send me forthwith into the house if I went near her."

" Then find Miss Betty and read her a page in the primer. You know you promised your father you would learn to read it correctly against his return."

" Betty is gossiping in the garret chamber with Sally Tracy ; surely I must stop with you, Biddy, dear ; " and Moppet twined her arms around Miss Bidwell's neck, with her little coaxing face upraised for a kiss. When Moppet said "Biddy dear" (which was her baby abbreviation for the old servant), she became irresistible : so Miss Bidwell, much relieved at dropping so puzzling a theological question as the propriety of supplications for the wellbeing of his Satanic majesty, proposed that she should tell Miss Moppet " a story," which met with delighted assent from the little girl.

Miss Bidwell's stories, which dated back for many years and always began with " when I was a little maid," were never failing in interest, besides being somewhat lengthy, as Moppet insisted upon minute detail, and invariably corrected her when

she chanced to omit the smallest particular.
That the story had been often told did not
make it lose any of its interest, and the
shadows of the great elm which overhung
the sitting-room windows grew longer, while
the sun sank lower and lower unheeded,
until Miss Bidwell, at the most thrilling
part of her tale, where a bloodthirsty and
evil-minded Indian was about to appear, suddenly laid down her work and exclaimed : —

" Hark! surely there is some one coming
up the back path," and rising as she spoke,
she hurried out to the side porch, closely
followed by Moppet, who said to herself,
with all a child's vivid and dramatic imagination, " Perhaps it 's an Indian coming to
tomahawk us in our beds!'" which thought
caused her to seize a fold of Miss Bidwell's
gown tightly in her hand.

As they came into the hall they were
joined by Miss Euphemia, who had also
heard the sounds of approach; and as they
emerged from the house two tall figures,
dusty and travel-worn, confronted them, with
Reuben following in their rear.

" Oliver!" exclaimed Miss Euphemia, as
she recognized her youngest nephew in one
of the wayfarers, " whence come you, and

MISS EUPHEMIA MEETS OLIVER AND HIS PRISONER

what news? Where is your honored father?"

"My father, madam," said Oliver Wolcott, uncovering his head as he motioned to Reuben to take his place near his companion, "my father is some thirty miles behind me, but hastening in this direction. What news?—Fairfield burnt, half its inhabitants homeless, but Tryon's marauders put to flight and our men in pursuit."

"And who is this gentleman?" said Miss Euphemia, as Oliver kissed her cheek and stepped back.

"'T is more than I can answer," said Oliver, "for not one word concerning himself can I obtain from him. He is my prisoner, Aunt Euphemia; I found him lurking in the woods ten miles away this morning, and should perhaps have let him pass had not a low-lying branch of a tree knocked off his hat, when I recognized him for one of Tryon's crew."

"Speak more respectfully, sir," said the stranger suddenly, "to me, if not to those whom you term 'Tryon's crew.'"

"I grant the respect due your arm and strength," said Oliver, "for you came near leaving me in the smoke and din of Fairfield when you gave me this blow," and he touched the left side of his head, where could be seen some clotted blood among his hair. "Come, sir, my aunt has asked the question. Do you not reply to a lady?"

"The gibe is unworthy of you," said the other, lifting the hat which had been drawn down closely over his brow; and I " —

"Oh, Oliver, 't is my good kind gentleman!" cried Moppet, darting forward and seizing the stranger by the hand; "he plunged into Great Pond last night and pulled me forth when I was nearly drowning, and we begged him to come home with us, did we not, Betty?" — seeing her sister standing in the doorway. "Betty, Betty, come and tell Oliver he has made a mistake."

A smile lit up the stranger's handsome face as he bowed low to Betty, who came swiftly to his side as she recognized him.

"Will you not bring the gentleman in, Oliver?" she said. "The thanks which are his due can hardly be well spoken on our doorstep," and Betty drew herself up, and waved her hand like the proud little maid she was, her eyes sparkling, her breast heaving with the excitement she strove to suppress.

Oliver looked from Moppet to Betty, in be-
wilderment then back at his prisoner, who
seemed the most unconcerned of the group.

"You are right, Betty," said Miss Euphemia, beginning to understand the situation. "Will you walk in, sir, and let me
explain to my nephew how greatly we are
indebted to you?" And she led the way
into the mansion, the others following, and
opened the door of the parlor on the left,
Reuben, obedient to a sign from Oliver,
remaining with Miss Bidwell in the hall.

The stranger declined the chair which
Oliver courteously offered him, and remained
standing near Betty, Moppet clinging to his
hand and looking up gratefully into his
face while Miss Euphemia related to her
nephew the story of Moppet's rescue from
her perilous accident of the previous day.

"A brave deed!" cried Oliver impetu-
ously, as he advanced with outstretched
hand toward his prisoner, "and with all my
heart, sir, I thank you. Forgive my pet-
tish speech of a moment since; you were
right to reprove me. No one appreciates a
gallant foe more than I; and though the
fortune of war has to-day made you my prisoner, to-morrow may make me yours."

"I thank you," said the stranger, giving his hand as frankly in return. "Believe me, my plunge in the pond was hardly worth the stress you are kind enough to lay upon it, and but for the mischance to my little friend here," smiling at Miss Moppet, who regarded him with affectionate eyes, "is an affair of little moment. May I ask where you will bestow me for the night, and also the privilege of a dip in cold water, as I am too soiled and travel-worn to sit in the presence of ladies, even though your prisoner."

"Prisoner!" echoed Betty, with a start. "Surely, Oliver, you will not hold as a prisoner the man who saved our little Moppet's life, and that, too (though he makes so light of it) at the risk of his own?"

"You will let him go free, brother Oliver," cried Moppet, flying to the young officer's side; "you surely will not clap him into jail?"

"It was my purpose," said Oliver, looking from one to the other, "to confine you until to-morrow and then carry you to head-quarters, where General Putnam will determine your ultimate fate. I certainly recognize you as the author of this cut on my head. Do you belong to the British army or are you a volunteer accompanying Tryon in his raid upon our innocent and unoffending neighbors at Fairfield?"

"Sir," said the other haughtily, "I pardon much to your youthful patriotism, which looks upon us as invaders. My name is Geoffrey Yorke, and I have the honor to bear his majesty's commission as captain in the Sixty-fourth Regiment of Foot."

Betty gave a faint exclamation. Oliver Wolcott stepped forward.

"Captain Yorke," he said, "I regret more than I can say my inability, which you yourself will recognize, to bid you go forth free and in safety. My duty is unfortunately but too plain. I, sir, serve the Continental Congress, and like you hold a captain's commission. I should be false alike to my country and my oath of allegiance did I permit you to escape; but there is one favor I can offer you: give me your parole, and allow me and my family the pleasure of holding you as a guest, not prisoner, while under our roof."

Geoffrey Yorke hesitated; he opened his lips to speak, when some instinct made him glance at Betty, who stood directly behind her brother. Her large, soft eyes were fixed

on his with most beseeching warning, and
she raised her dainty finger to her lips as
she slowly, almost imperceptibly, shook her
head.

"Captain Wolcott," he said, "I fully
appreciate your kindness and the motive
which prompts it. I have landed on these
shores but one short month ago, and Sir
Henry Clinton ordered me — but these par-
ticulars will not interest you. I thank you
for your offer, but I decline to take parole,
and prefer instead the fortunes of war."

"Then, sir, I have no choice," said Oliver.
"Aunt Euphemia, will you permit me to
use the north chamber? I will conduct you
there, Captain Yorke, and shall see that you
are well guarded for the night." And with
a courtly bow to the ladies Geoffrey Yorke
followed his captor from the room, as Moppet threw herself into Betty's arms and
sobbed bitterly.

CHAPTER IV

FRIEND OR FOE

BETTY WOLCOTT sat alone in her own room, thinking intently. The windows were all open, and the soft night air blew the dainty curls off her white forehead and disclosed the fact of her very recent tears. Never, in all her short, happy life, had Betty been so moved as now, for the twin passions of gratitude and loyalty were at war within her, and she realized, with a feeling akin to dismay, that she must meet the responsibility alone, that those of her household were all arrayed against her.

" If my father were but at home," said Betty to herself, " he would know and understand, but Oliver will not listen, no, not even when I implored him to keep Captain Yorke close prisoner here for two days, by which time my father is sure to arrive. Aunt Euphemia is too timid and Pamela is much the same : as Josiah happens to agree perfectly with Oliver, Pamela could never

be induced to see how cruel it is to repay
our debt in this way.   Oliver is but a boy,"
— and Betty's lips curved in scorn over her
brother's four years' seniority, — " and —
and — oh! I am, indeed, astray.   What,
here I am, one of the loyal Wolcotts, — a
family known all through the land as true
to the cause of Freedom and the Declara-
tion, — and here I sit planning how to let a
British officer, foe to my country, escape
from my father's house.   I wonder the walls
do not open and fall on me," and poor Betty
gazed half fearfully overhead, as if she expected the rafters would descend upon the
author of such treasonable sentiments.   " But
something must be done," she thought rapidly.   " I care not whether he be friend or
foe, I take the consequences; be mine the
blame," and she lifted her pretty head with
an air of determination, as a soft knock fell
upon her chamber door; but before she
could rise to open it, the latch was raised
and a little figure, all in white, crept inside.

" I can't sleep, Betty," sobbed Moppet,
as her sister gathered the child in her arms;
" it 's too, too dreadful.   Will General Putnam hang my dear, kind gentleman as the

British hanged Captain Nathan Hale, and shall we never, never see him more?"

"Dear heart," said Betty, smoothing the yellow hair, and tears springing again to her eyes as she thought of the brave, manly face of her country's foe. "No, Moppet, Captain Yorke is not a spy, as, alas! was poor Nathan Hale, but"—

"Betty," whispered Moppet, so low that she was evidently alarmed at her own daring, "why can't we let him go free and never tell Oliver a word about it?"

"How did you come to think of that?" said Betty, astonished.

"I am afraid it is the devil prompting me," said Moppet, with a sigh, partly over her own iniquity, and part in wonderment as to whether that overworked personage was somewhere soaring in the air near at hand; "but I always thought the British were big ogres, with fierce eyes and red whiskers, and I am sure my good, kind gentleman is very like ourselves."

Betty was betrayed into a low laugh. Moppet was always original, but this was delicious.

"No, child," she said softly, "the British are some bad, some good, and there are no

doubt cruel men to be found in all wars.
Moppet, as you came by the north door,
whom did you see on guard in the hall?"

"Josiah Huntington," said Moppet
promptly; "but you heard what Oliver said
at supper?"

"Yes," answered Betty, "Oliver was so
weary that Josiah was to watch until twelve
o'clock: then, at midnight, Reuben was to
guard the hall until four in the morning,
when Oliver would take his place until
breakfast. Did you note the time on the
hall clock?"

"It was half past eleven," said Moppet:
"the half hour sounded as I rapped."

Betty sat pondering for a moment, then
she slid Moppet gently from her lap to the
floor and rose.

"Moppet," she said gravely, "you are a
little maid, but you have a true heart, and I
believe you can keep a secret. I am going
to try to release Captain Yorke, and I
think you can help me. I bind you to keep
silent, except to our dear and honored father, and even to him you shall not speak
until I permit you. Promise me, dear
heart?"

"I promise," said Moppet solemnly, and

Betty knew that, no matter what happened, she could depend on her devoted little sister.

"Moppet," said Betty, "I have a plan, but 't is a slender one. Do you recollect how close the great elm-tree boughs come to your window?"

"I can put out my hand and nearly reach them," said Moppet; "you remember Reuben cut the bough nearest, but oh, Betty, the tree has a limb which runs an arm's length only from the north chamber."

"So I thought," answered Betty, who was busily engaged in changing her light summer gown for one of homespun gray; "and now, Moppet, you and I must go into your room for the next part of my plot. I must speak to Captain Yorke, and can you guess how I shall manage to do it?"

Moppet's eyes grew large and round with excitement. "I know," she whispered breathlessly, "through my doll's dungeon. Oh, Betty, how lucky 't is that Oliver never once dreamed of that!"

"I doubt if he even knows its existence," said Betty. "There goes the clock," as the slow, solemn voice of the timepiece sounded out on the night. "It is twelve o'clock, and Reuben will be coming upstairs

from the kitchen.   Hark! " — extinguishing
her candle and opening her door softly.
" Josiah has gone to the turn on the stairs,
and is speaking to Reuben ; quick, Moppet,
if you come still as a mouse they will not
see us before we can gain your door," and
with swift, soft steps the two small figures
stole across the hall in the semi-darkness
which the night lamp standing near the
great clock but served to make visible, and
in another second, panting and eager, they
stood safely within Moppet's chamber, clinging to each other, as they quickly fastened
the latch.

Moppet's chamber was a small one, and
occupied the centre of the house, Miss Euphemia's being upon one side, and the north
chamber (as one of the great rooms was
called) upon the other.   The great chimney
of the mansion ran up between the large and
small room, and what Moppet called her
" doll's dungeon " was a hollow place, just
high enough for the child to reach, in the
back of the chimney.   For some purpose of
ventilation there was an opening from this
aperture into the north chamber.   It was
covered with a piece of movable iron ; and
in summer, when no fire was used in that

part of the house, Moppet took great delight in consigning her contumacious doll (a rag baby of large size and much plainness of feature) to what she was pleased to call her "dungeon." To-night Betty's quick wit had divined what an important factor the aperture might prove to her, and directly she had secured the door, she walked softly toward the chimney, and felt in the darkness for the movable bit of iron which filled the back.

When Geoffrey Yorke had finished the ample and delicious supper with which Miss Euphemia's hospitable and pitying soul had furnished him, he lighted his candle and made thorough search of his temporary prison to ascertain whether he could escape therefrom. Betty's gesture of disapproval when he was about to give his parole had seemed to promise him assistance; could it be possible that the lovely little rebel's heart was so moved with pity?"

"Sweet Betty," thought Geoffrey, "was ever maid so grateful for a small service! I wish with all my soul I might have chance and opportunity to do her a great one, for never have I seen so bewitching and dainty a creature," and Geoffrey's heart gave a

mad leap as he remembered the tearful, beseeching glance which Betty had bestowed
upon him as Oliver had conducted him from
her presence.

The windows, of which there were two,
looking north, received his first attention, but
he found them amply secured; and although
a strong arm might wrench them open, it
would be attended by such noise as could
not fail to attract the attention of his guard
posted outside the door. This reflection
prompted him to inspect the door; and dis-
covering an inside bolt as well as the outer
one, he drew it, thus assuring his privacy
from intrusion. The large chimney was his
next point of investigation; and although the
flue seemed somewhat narrow, Geoffrey decided that it afforded some slight chance,
provided he had the means of descent when
once he reached the roof. Back to the windows again; yes, the great elm of which
Moppet had spoken stood like a tall sentinel
guarding the mansion, and Geoffrey felt
confident that he could crawl from roof to
tree and thus reach the ground. To be sure,
it was most hazardous; there was the chance
of some one sleeping in the chambers near
who might hear even so slight a noise; he

might become wedged in the chimney, or —
pshaw! one must risk life, if need be, for
liberty ; and here Geoffrey smiled, as it occurred to him that this was what these very
colonists were engaged in doing, and for a
moment the British officer felt a throb of
sympathy hitherto unknown to him. He
had landed at New York but a month before, filled with insular prejudices and con-
tempt for these country lads and farmers,
whom he imagined composed the Continental
army ; but the fight at Fairfield, which was
carried on by the Hessians with a brutality
that disgusted him. and the encounter with
such a family as this under whose roof he
was, began to open his eyes, and he acknow-
leged frankly to himself that young Oliver
Wolcott was both a soldier and a gentleman.

"The boy looked every inch a soldier,"
thought Geoffrey, "when he refused his sister's pleading ; faith, he is made of firm stuff
to withstand her. Oh, Betty, Betty ! I wonder if the fortunes of war will ever let me
see your face again," and with a sigh com-
pounded of many things, Geoffrey picked
up a book that was lying on the table, and
resolved to read until it should be far on

into the night, when he would make a bold
attempt to escape.

The clock on the stairs struck twelve, and
Geoffrey, roused from the light slumber into
which he had fallen, heard the steps outside
his door as Josiah Huntington was joined
by Reuben, who was to relieve his guard,
and straightened himself, with a long breath,
as he rose from his chair. As he did so, he
became conscious of a slight, very slight,
noise in the direction of the chimney; and
turning his eyes toward it, a soft whisper
reached his ear.

"Captain Yorke," murmured the sweetest
voice in the world; and as the slight grating
noise ceased, to his amazement a little white
hand beckoned him to approach a small
aperture, which he now perceived in the
bricks about four feet from the floor. Very
softly Geoffrey obeyed the summons, and
cautiously made his way to the chimney.

"Kneel down and put your ear near me,"
said Betty, and the tall soldier dropped on
one knee obediently; "be very careful, for
though Aunt Euphemia's chamber is on this
side, and she is usually a sound sleeper, it
might be our ill fortune that to-night she
would wake. I have made up my mind,

sir; I cannot keep you prisoner under a roof that but for you might be mourning my little sister dead."

"I pray you say no more of that," interrupted Geoffrey softly. "I am more than repaid by your interest in my unhappy condition."

"It may be wrong, it doubtless is," said Betty, sighing, "but I have two plans for your escape. Tell me, are your windows securely fastened?"

"Too strongly to be tampered with except by making noise that is certain to be overheard," returned Geoffrey.

"Then we must try other means; if you can but manage to scale the chimney, — and I think there are still some pegs inside which Reuben put there in the spring when he went up after burning it out, — if you can reach the roof by the chimney you will find on the south side, close to the chimney itself, a trap-door which lets down by a ladder into our garret. The ladder is stationary, and I will meet you there at its foot, and from the garret there is a back stairway, down which you may creep to the buttery, and once there 't is but a step outside when I open the door."

"God bless you," whispered Geoffrey, feeling a mad desire to kiss the pretty pink ear and soft cheek which he could just see by the dim light of Miss Moppet's candle; "shall I start at once?"

"No," returned Betty, "Josiah Huntington has but just sought his chamber, and he will be watchful. Wait until you hear the old clock on the staircase strike three; that is the hour, I have been told, when all sleep most soundly. Then Moppet will tell you if all goes right, for I shall be waiting for you, as I said, above;" and with a soft "be very, very careful to make no noise," Betty moved away from the "doll's dungeon" and Yorke bounded to his feet.

"Now, Moppet," said Betty softly, "let me wrap you well in your woolen habit, lest you take cold."

"Oh, Betty darling," whispered the child, "how will you ever gain the garret stairs when Reuben is watching? He will be sure to think it strange; can I not go for you?"

"No, never," said Betty tenderly. "I will slip by Reuben, and you must not fret. Sit here on my knee and go fast asleep until I wake you."

Moppet nestled her little head down obe-

diently on Betty's shoulder; but try hard
though she did to keep her eyes wide open,
sleep at last overcame her, — sleep so profound after all this excitement that Betty
was able to lay her softly upon her bed
without awaking, and for the remainder of
those long hours Betty kept her vigil alone.
It was nervous work; for determined though
she was to release Yorke, Betty possessed a
most sensitive and tender conscience, and
love for her country and her people was as
the air she breathed. It proved the tena-
city of her purpose and the strength of her
will that, notwithstanding her many misgiv-
ings, when she heard the clock sound the
quarter she rose from her low seat by the
window, where she had been gazing out into
the night, and whispered softly to Moppet
that it was time to wake. The child sprang
up, alert and quick as Betty herself, and
listened to her sister's last warning instructions to have no fear, but wait quietly for
her return, and when the clock struck the
hour to whisper through the hole in the
chimney to Yorke that she had gone.

Very softly, her slippers held tightly in
her hand, Betty pulled up the latch of the
bedroom door and stepped into the almost

dark hall. The night lamp had partly died
out, but there was still enough of its flickering light to permit her, when her eyes grew
accustomed to it, to see the dim outline of
Reuben's figure sitting on a stool at the
door of the north chamber. In order to
reach the garret from this part of the house
she must go directly down the hall to where
it parted at the L, where the stairs reaching
the garret were shut off by a door, on the
other side of which was a square landing,
where you could turn down and descend
directly from the garret to the buttery.
Once past Reuben, she would feel comparatively safe, for although Oliver's room
was opposite he was too weary to be wakeful. It took scarcely a minute to creep
toward Reuben, and Betty drew a quick
breath of relief when she perceived that the
farmer-bred lad, unaccustomed to night
watches, and feeling that his prisoner was
secure behind the bolted door, had fallen
fast asleep. Another minute and she had
fairly flown through the hall and reached
the door of the garret stairs ; she recollected
that the latch had a troublesome creak occasionally ; indeed, she had noticed it only that
very day, as she and Sally Tracy had

mounted to their eyrie in the big dormer
window of the garret, where safe from all
ears they were wont to confide their girlish
secrets to each other.

" Pray Heaven it creak not to-night," said
Betty to herself as she gently and steadily
pulled the handle of the latch and saw the
dreaded door open to her hand. Inside
stepped Betty, and made breathless pause
while she closed it, and the amiable latch
fell softly down again into its place. Swift
as a flash the girlish figure flitted up the
winding narrow stairs, and gasping but triumphant Betty seated herself on the lowest
step of the trap-ladder to await the coming
of Geoffrey Yorke.

In the bedroom below, Miss Moppet, whose
soul was thrilling with mingled delight and
terror at being an actor in a " real story,"
waited as she was told until she heard the
deep voice of the clock, sounding rather
more awful than usual, say " one, two,
three ! " and then tiptoeing over the bare
floor she opened with small trembling fingers the tiny aperture and whispered, " Are
you there ? " starting back half frightened
as the instant answer came, close beside her :

" Yes, is it time ? "

"Betty is in the garret by now," she faltered. "Oh, sir, be careful and fare you well!"

For answer Geoffrey Yorke bent down, and taking the small cold fingers extended to him, pressed a kiss on them, and with a soft "farewell" began his passage up the chimney.

It was no such very difficult task he found, to his satisfaction, for Betty was right, and by feeling carefully with his hands he perceived the friendly pegs which Reuben had inserted, and of which Oliver had no knowledge, else he would not have trusted so agile and strong a prisoner within their reach. Geoffrey's broad shoulders were the only sufferers, but the rough home-spun which covered them was a better pro-tection than his uniform would have been, and he again blessed the good fortune which had thrown the disguise in his way as he left Fairfield four days before.

Betty, sitting on the ladder step, straining her ears to catch the first sound, became conscious of a light bound as Geoffrey swung himself from the chimney top to the roof, and she sped up the ladder to unhook the door of the trap just as he reached it.

"Speak not a word," she said in his ear, as he set his foot on the ladder, "but fasten the hook lest they discover that the door has been opened. Now, give me your hand," and in the darkness the strong, manly hand closed firmly over her dainty fingers with a clasp which, strangely enough, inspired her with fresh courage.

"Stop," said Betty suddenly, as they were at the top stair, "you must remove your boots; the slightest creak might wake the sleepers at the end of the hall."

It took but a second of time to follow her directions; and then very softly, with many pauses, the pair crept down the winding stairs, and Betty involuntarily held her breath until the last step was safely passed and she raised the latch of the buttery door.

"If Miss Bidwell has locked it," came the swift thought, — but, no! like everything else that dreadful night, fortune seeemed to favor Betty, and with a long-drawn sigh she drew her companion across the threshold and instantly shot the bolt behind her.

A faint glow of dawn crept through the pantry windows, and Betty paused a moment and regarded the rows of milk pans which adorned the shelves of the small room with grave intentness.

"Had you not better take a glass of milk?" she said. "You may have to travel far without food, although I am sure that should you ask for it at any of our Connecticut farmhouses you would be cheerfully supplied," and raising the neat dipper she filled it and handed it to Geoffrey, who took it gratefully from her hand.

"And now put on your boots, for freedom lies beyond that door," she said, still in softest tones, as she unbolted the other door which led directly outside. "I must go with you as far as the barn, for you will need my mare to take you out of danger of pursuit."

"No, no," answered Geoffrey, speaking for the first time as they sped rapidly over the grass, "I will not take her; you have dared much for me, and I fear censure and harm may come to you for releasing me should you be discovered."

"Censure," said Betty, throwing back her small head haughtily, "wherefore? Do you think I shall conceal my share in this night's work? Oliver is but a hot-headed boy: had my father been at home it would have been different, and to him I shall make my confession, that I have given liberty to — oh, I cannot say a foe, after what you have done for me — to a British officer who comes to slay my countrymen ! "

" Never your foe, Betty," cried Yorke, confronting her with face as pale as her own, and in his admiration of her spirit and nobility forgetting all else. " Say, rather, your adoring friend, who one day, God willing, hopes to prove to you that there are British hearts which are true and honest as yours, and that none will be more loyal to you than mine own."

A hot wave of color flashed up over Betty's charming face; her lips trembled, but no words came from them. What was this impetuous young man daring to say to her?

" The dawn is breaking over yonder hills," Geoffrey rushed on, " and before the sun rises I must be as many miles away as my feet can carry me. Farewell, farewell ! — may God bless and keep you always. Go back straightway into the mansion ; I shall not stir step until I see you safe." And through her brimming tears Betty realized that his kisses were falling on her hands, as without a word she turned and fled toward

the open door. But when she reached it
some new-born impulse tearing madly at her
heart made her pause, and looking back she
saw Geoffrey lift something from the grass
at his feet which he waved toward her as he
sped down the path, and raising her hand to
her gown she knew that he had carried with
him her breast-knot of rose-colored ribbon.

CHAPTER V

A LOYAL TRAITOR

BETTY stumbled blindly over the threshold, and with shaking fingers secured the outer bolt of the buttery door. Her head was whirling, and she dared not stop there even to think over this extraordinary adventure, for Moppet was doubtless waiting breathlessly for her return; and at the recollection Betty's nerves grew steadier, and she bethought herself that a glass of milk would be needed by the child and that she must take it to her. So she filled the smallest dipper, not wishing to go back into the china pantry for fear of noise, and, with the milk in hand, concluded it was wiser to seek the main staircase in the hall, rather than wake Reuben by drawing his attention to the exit on the garret stairway. And fortunate it was for Betty that she had so determined; for as she set her foot upon the first step of the stairs, she beheld Oliver leaning over the upper balustrade, gazing gravely down upon her.

"Good-morning," said Betty readily, in a cheerful undertone, as she reached his side; "you are up betimes, Oliver."

"Where have you been?" asked her brother.

"To the buttery," said Betty: "this is milk for Moppet. The child is wakeful, and needs it."

"Why did you not send Reuben?" asked Oliver, who was always kind and attentive to his sisters.

"Reuben?" echoed Betty. "Did you not set him as guard to your prisoner?" and then, her heart smiting her for the gibe, "Miss Bidwell lets no one meddle with her milk pans, and I knew best which were last night's milk," and she went up the hall with a naughty little throb of mingled mischief and triumph, as she thought how she had outwitted him, while the unsuspecting Oliver seated himself near the north chamber door.

Moppet, sitting up in bed, welcomed her sister with open arms, and drank the milk thirstily, as Betty told her that all was safe, and that Captain Yorke was now well on his way.

" I 'm as glad as can be," said Moppet, who was troubled with no conscientious scruples whatever, and was now beginning to enjoy herself intensely at sharing a mystery with Betty; "I told him you were gone, after the big clock struck three, and oh, Betty, he kissed my hand through the hole in the chimney."

" Did he?" said Betty, flushing brightly under Moppet's keen glance.

" And I sat there and shivered," went on Moppet, discreetly dropping that branch of the subject, " for I could hear his feet as he climbed, and once he slipped, and I was so frightened lest he should come tumbling down and our fine plot be discovered. Betty, Betty, what a fine flutter Oliver and Josiah will be in at breakfast!"

" Don't talk of it," said Betty, shivering in her turn; "go to sleep, Moppet, and I will fly to my chamber, for it is not well that I should be discovered here, dressed. Oliver is not one to notice; now lie still until you are called for rising;" and Betty tripped back to her own room, where, tearing off her dress, she threw her tired little self on the bed to rest, if not to sleep, for the short hours that remained before breakfast.

The Wolcott household was one that was
early astir, however, and Chloe, the old colored cook, was out in the barn searching for
eggs, and Miss Bidwell had laid the breakfast cloth and polished the silver by half
past six, when Miss Euphemia knocked
briskly at the door where Pamela and Dolly
Trumbull were slumbering sweetly, and resolved that she would request Oliver to
permit Captain Yorke to come down and
breakfast with the family. " For," mused
Miss Euphemia, " our obligations to that
young man should make some difference, I
think, in his treatment; I must try to persuade Oliver to detain him here until my
brother's return, for although I did not think
it prudent to say so, I confess I am no more
anxious to keep him prisoner than Betty
was."

But Miss Euphemia had not more than
descended at half past seven precisely (her
usual hour) when Oliver came hastily into
the room, demanding a hammer and chisel,
and with such evident dismay upon his
countenance that Miss Euphemia asked if
anything was the matter.

" I do not know," said Oliver, searching
the drawer for the desired implements; " I

called and knocked smartly at Captain
Yorke's door to ask him if he desired hot
water, and to offer him a change of clean
linen (as we are much the same size and
build) ; but although I made sufficient noise
to wake the hardest sleeper, no response did
I receive. Then I unbolted the door, intending to enter, but he has fastened it on the
inside, and " —

" He is ill," cried Miss Euphemia, in
alarm. " I noted he looked pale last night."

" Much more likely 't is some device to
alarm us," said Oliver, seizing the chisel,
and Miss Euphemia followed him as he
went hurriedly up the front staircase. At
its top stood Huntington.

" Captain Yorke is a sound sleeper," he
said, addressing Oliver. " I have knocked at
his door several times and get no response."

" My mind misgives me," said Oliver, fitting his chisel in the door and striking vig-
orously with the hammer ; " and yet I made
sure there was no chance for escape, — ha ! "
as the door swung open and discovered the
closed shutters and the last flickering gleams
of the dying candle upon the table. " Good
heavens, Huntington, he has flown ! "

" Flown ! " cried Josiah, rushing after

Oliver, as Miss Euphemia joined the party,
and Pamela, with Dolly, opened her door
across the hall, hearing the commotion.
" And how? Surely not by the chimney?"

" I wish you had suggested that earlier,"
said Oliver bitterly.   " I am a dolt and a
fool's head not to have thoroughly exam-
ined it last night," and he rushed across
into Betty's chamber to find a candle with
which to investigate the treacherous exit.

" Have a care, Oliver," cried Betty, as
her brother entered without knocking, to
find her with her hair over her shoulders,
brush in hand. " What do you please to
want ? "

" Your candle," said Oliver, catching up
the one upon her table, and then pausing, as
he was about to rush out again. " Did you
hear any noises last night, Betty ? "

" Noises ? " answered Betty, facing him
calmly, " of what nature ? "

" In the great chimney," said Oliver,
eying her sternly.

" I did not," said Betty, with truth, returning inward thanks that to that question
she could reply without falsehood. " Why
did you ask?"

" You will find out soon enough," said

Oliver, dashing down the hall, without closing the door, and hurrying to the kitchen for a light. By the time he returned, he found Josiah half way up the chimney.

" Here are pegs," he called out, as Oliver sent the ray of the lighted candle upward. " 'T is easy enough to see how our prisoner escaped. Fool that I was not to have searched this place," and he let himself down again, where the bewildered group stood around the chimney-piece.

"The fault is mine alone," cried Oliver furiously ; " let us get out on the roof and see if we can discover how he made his descent to the ground."

" By the great elm," exclaimed Pamela, who had unfastened the shutters with Josiah's help ; " see, the branches overhang the roof just here, and I think there are some pieces of the bark on the ground below." All of which was true, and quickwitted of Pamela ; but Moppet could have explained the presence of the bits of bark, for, as it happened, the child had emptied her apron under the elm the day before, and the bark was some she had gathered in the orchard for the bits of fungus which, at night, were phosphorescent, and which Moppet called " fairy lamps."

"True," said Josiah, leaning out of the window, "and there are footsteps in the tall grass yonder," pointing westward, where his keen eye perceived a fresh path broken in the meadow. "I must follow Oliver to the roof; this will be a dire blow to him, as he thought his prisoner so carefully guarded."

"How clever of him to escape under our very ears," said Dolly to Pamela; "how could Captain Yorke contrive to climb down so softly that no one heard him? Is not Miss Euphemia's chamber on this side?"

"Yes," said Pamela, turning away from the window, "and so is Moppet's; where is Aunt Euphemia?" and running out into the hall, she encountered both Betty and her aunt on the way to Moppet's apartment.

"Hush!" whispered Betty, with hand on the latch, "I hope she is still sleeping. Moppet came into my room in the night, Aunt Euphemia, and was so cold and shivering that I went back with her and put her to bed. I got a drink of milk for her, and it seemed to quiet her."

"That was quite right," said Miss Euphemia. "I have been afraid that the plunge in the pond did her some injury."

and she opened the door softly, only to see Miss Moppet's curly head rise up from her pillow, and to hear her say with a sleepy yawn : —

" What is it all about? Where 's Betty?"

" Here I am," said Betty, giving her a kiss. " Did you sleep soundly after the milk ? "

" Yes, and I want some more," said Moppet, seizing the situation with such alacrity that Betty suspected on the instant that the keen little ears had been on the alert for more minutes than Moppet cared to acknowledge. " What are you all coming in for? Is it dinner-time ? "

" No," interrupted Pamela, " we have not even had breakfast. Captain Yorke has escaped in the night" —

" Escaped ! " cried Moppet, the liveliest curiosity in her tone. " Oh, I 'm so glad! Are n't you, Betty? "

" Better not let Oliver hear you say that," said Pamela in an undertone as Miss Euphemia drew Betty aside.

" How did he get out? " said Moppet, giving way to laughter. " Oh, what a ruffle Oliver must be in."

" Naughty child," said Pamela, but unable

to help smiling at Moppet's view of the situation. "Did you happen to hear any noises on the roof or in the big elm last night?"

"Not a sound," said Moppet, like Betty rejoicing inwardly that she could reply truthfully, for the little maid had never told a lie in her short life, and had indeed spent a wakeful half hour that very morning wondering how she would be able to evade any questions that might be put to her. "Did Captain Yorke climb out of his window and go down the big elm, Pamela? Do you know I thought of that at supper."

"He could not open the window, Moppet," answered Pamela, "but he did go down the tree from the roof, whence he climbed from the chimney here."

"Moppet, you must instantly dress or you will take cold," said Miss Euphemia, interrupting, to Betty's relief, "and I will be glad if Betty will assist you, for I must go down and see if breakfast be still hot, as no one is ready yet to eat it," and out went Miss Euphemia, calling the others to follow her.

"What do you think of all this?" asked Pamela of Betty.

"What do you suppose?" flashed out

Betty, whose quick tongue had been so long restrained that it was absolute relief to her to speak her mind. " I am as glad as I can possibly be that Captain Yorke has escaped, and if that be disloyal " — finished the spirited little maid, mindful of Patrick Henry — " make the most of it ! "

" Oh, Betty ! " cried Pamela, shocked beyond expression.

" It is I that should be shocked, not you," went on Betty. " Do you hold Moppet's dear life as nothing ? Do you not wish to acknowledge an obligation when it is doubly due ? I am ashamed of you, Pamela, — you and Oliver. I would my father were here to make you see both sides of a question clearly."

" Betty, Betty," implored Pamela, bursting into tears, " do I not love our little sister as well as you ? You do mistake me ; I did not dare go counterwise to Oliver and Josiah, but indeed I love you for your courage."

" There, say no more," said Betty, dropping the brush with which she was reducing Moppet's rebellious locks to order, and rushing into Pamela's arms with quick repentance. " I am cross and upset this morning.

and not fit to talk to you, my gentle Pamela,
so go down and make the coffee and forgive
my petulance."

Dolly, who had witnessed this little sisterly passage of arms in shy fright, put her
hand in Pamela's and whispered, as they
gained the staircase : —

"Dry your eyes, Pamela dear : Betty is
most forward to speak thus to her elder sister."

"There you mistake," said Pamela, changing front with true feminine inconsistency.
"Betty is quite right, and I am displeased,
— yes downright displeased with myself that
I did not side with her last night," and with
unwonted color flushing her usually pale
cheeks Pamela walked into the breakfast-
room, Dolly following meekly behind her.

Meanwhile, Oliver and Josiah were upon
the roof of the mansion conducting most
careful investigation.   They had decided
that it was useless to pursue Yorke, for he
might have many hours in advance of them,
and they must take the chances that he
would be recaptured by some of Putnam's
men, especially if he again mistook the
country and went west instead of north.
They climbed through the trap-door, but as

the heavy dews had not yet begun there was
no trace of footsteps upon the roof beyond a
faint mark, which might be the spot where
the prisoner had dropped from the chimney.
It was quite possible for an agile fellow,
accustomed to use his muscle, to clamber
down the sloping roof to the elm and escape
to the ground by its branches, and that he
was not heard was partly due to his own
care and the unusually heavy slumbers of
the inmates of the mansion. Having reached
this conclusion, Oliver was fain to make the
best of it, and in much chagrin descended
to the breakfast-table.

Try as she did to look demure and avoid
speaking upon the subject which all were
discussing, Betty could not keep her dancing eyes in order, and before the meal was
over she flashed so roguish a glance at Oliver that, irritated at her mute opposition, he
could not refrain from saying: —

" There sits Betty looking fairly pleased
because she has her own way, and apparently cares nothing for the escape of an
enemy to her country."

" Fie, Oliver," spoke up Pamela with
unusual fire, " Betty is as loyal as you or I,
and you are unfair to tax her because she

heartily disapproves of your course in regard
to Captain Yorke's detention after the sig-
nal service he has rendered to all us Wolcotts."

"Pamela!" cried Oliver, good temper
returning, and gazing in comic dismay at
his favorite sister, much as he would at a
dove who had ruffled its plumes. "This
from you, Pamela? If Betty be allowed to
demoralize the family in this wise, I think
it were well my father takes you all in
hand."

"Heyday?" said a kindly voice from the
door of the sitting-room, as a fine-looking
man dressed in the Continental uniform
entered the room. "Who is it that requires
my parental hand, Oliver, and why do you
so lament my absence?"

"Father, father!" shrieked Miss Moppet, tumbling out of her chair and flinging
her arms around General Wolcott's neck as
he stooped down to embrace her. "Oh,
we're so glad you are come. Why did n't
you get here last night?"

"Because I lay over at General Putnam's
headquarters," said her father. "Oliver,
you will find Captain Seymour and Lieutenant Hillhouse on the porch. See that their

horses be taken and fed, and bid them come to breakfast."

Oliver disappeared in haste, and Josiah, with an apology to Miss Euphemia, followed him; while General Wolcott, casting off his hat and gloves, seated himself with Moppet on his knee, and Miss Bidwell appeared from the kitchen with fresh reinforcements of breakfast for the newcomers. Betty, busying herself by fetching cups and saucers from the china pantry, caught fragments of the conversation, and became aware that Miss Moppet was telling the story of her adventure at Great Pond, in the child's most dramatic fashion, and that Miss Euphemia was also adding her testimony to the tale as it went on. They were presently interrupted by the entrance of Oliver with his father's two aids, and the large mahogany table was surrounded by guests, whose appetites bid fair to do justice to Miss Bidwell's breakfast.

No sooner was the meal fairly under way than Oliver, eager to hear his father's opinion, began the story of his capture of the day before, and related how and where he had found Captain Yorke, and how safely he supposed he had imprisoned him in the

north chamber, from which his clever and
ready escape had been made. Oliver's nar-
rative was interrupted by exclamations from
the officers and questions from his father,
who displayed keen interest in the matter.

" Father," said Moppet, seeing that the
most important point had been omitted in
Oliver's story, and venturing to join in the
conversation, as few children of that period
would have done, " Oliver's prisoner was my
good kind gentleman who pulled me out of
the pond, and I am very, very glad he has
got away — are n't you ? "

" I was indeed hard bestead, sir," burst
in Oliver. " Here were Betty and Moppet
insisting that I must let Captain Yorke go
free because of his gallant act (which I
fully appreciate), and the gentleman refus-
ing his parole because he preferred to take
the chances of war, while I felt it my sworn
duty to detain him and to forward him to
General Putnam without delay, as I know
we are in need of exchange for several of
our officers now held by Sir Henry Clinton,
and this man is of Clinton's staff, and therefore a most valuable capture. Was I to
blame for retaining him ? "

General Wolcott hesitated, but as he was

about to make reply his eye fell upon Betty, who confronted him across the table with parted lips and large, beseeching eyes so full of entreaty that he changed the words almost upon his lips.

" It is a delicate question, my son," he said gravely, "and one I would rather not discuss at the present moment. More especially " — and a half-quizzical smile lit up his grave but kindly face as he turned toward Miss Moppet and gently pinched her little ear, — " more especially as the gentleman has taken the law in his own hands and escaped from Wolcott Manor despite the fact that as it is the residence of a Continental officer and the sheriff of Litchfield County it might be supposed to have exceptional reasons for detaining him. Captain Seymour, I will be glad to sign the papers of which General Putnam has need, and we will go at once to my library, for you must be off by noon."

Some two hours later, as Betty sat watching in her chamber window, she saw the horses led around to the front door, and shortly after knew from the sounds below that Pamela and Dolly were bidding the young officers good-by ; so, waiting until the sound of their horses' feet had died away in the distance, Betty, with outward composure but much inward dismay, tripped softly downstairs and knocked at the door of the library.

"Pray Heaven he be alone," she sighed as she heard her father's voice bid her enter, and then she crossed the threshold and confronted him.

"Father," she said, steadying herself by one small hand pressed downward on the table behind which he sat, " I — that is — I have something to tell you."

General Wolcott raised his head from the paper which he had been carefully reading and looked kindly at her.

"What is it, my child?" he asked reassuringly, motioning her to a chair. "I thought at breakfast that you had the air of being in distress."

"Nay, I am hardly that," replied Betty, clinging to the table, "except so far as I may have incurred your censure, though I hope not your displeasure. Father, Oliver has told you of the escape of Captain Yorke, which causes him much chagrin and anger. Blame no one but me, for I myself released him."

" You ! " exclaimed General Wolcott.

" Yes, I," said Betty, growing paler. " If you had but been here or I known that you were so near us, there had been no such need for haste, and I would have been spared this confession."

" How did you arrange the escape ? " said her father quietly.

" It was this way," faltered Betty, but gaining courage as she proceeded. " Oliver would not listen, though I begged and plead with him to delay until your arrival. He was so eager to deliver his captive to General Putnam that I made no impression. Father, the Englishman had saved our Moppet's life at the risk of his own ; *he* did not pause to ask whether she was friend or foe when he rushed to her rescue — could we be less humane ? I do not know what they do to prisoners," — and Betty strangled a swift sob, — but I could not bear to think of a gallant gentleman, be he British or American, confined in a prison, and so I resolved I would assist his escape. I waited until midnight, and then I spoke to him through the aperture in the great chimney and instructed him how to climb up through it by the pegs Reuben had left there, and I stole

to the garret and waited until he came.
Reuben did not see me pass the door of the
north chamber, for he was asleep (do not
tell this to Oliver, as it might bring reproof
upon poor Reuben, who was too weary to be
of much service as a sentinel), and I brought
Captain Yorke safely down the stairs which
lead from the garret to the buttery. Once
there, all was easy; I opened the door, and
— and — I even offered him the mare, father, I was in such fear of his recapture;
but he stoutly refused to take her. This is
all. If I am a traitor, dear father, punish
me as I deserve, but never think me disloyal
to you or to my country."

There was a pause, as Betty's sweet, passionate tones ceased; she stood with head
thrown back, but downcast eyes, as fair a
picture as ever greeted father's eye.

"A loyal traitor, Betty," said General
Wolcott slowly; "and I think that it were
well I should look after the condition of my
chimneys."

Scarcely daring to believe her ears, Betty
looked up, and in another second she had
thrown her arms around her father's neck,
sobbing softly as he caressed her.

"'T was a daring, mad scheme, my child,"

said General Wolcott, his own eyes not
quite guiltless of moisture; "but bravely
carried out; and looking at the matter
much as you do, I cannot find it in my heart
to censure you. Captain Yorke is doubtless
a manly foe, and of such I have no fear. It
shall be our secret, yours and mine, Betty;
we will not even tell Oliver just now, else it
might make sore feeling between you. For
Oliver was right, and "— smiling kindly,
"so were you. Everything depends upon
the point of view, my daughter; but let me
beg you never to try your hand again to
assist the escape of a British officer, or it
might cost me the friendship of General
Washington."

"Father, dear father!" cried Betty, overjoyed to find judgment so lenient accorded
her, "I crave your pardon; 't was alone for
Moppet's sake."

"Aye," said General Wolcott, and then
paused a brief second, for his wife's death
had been the forfeit paid for Moppet's
birth, and this was one reason why the child
had become the family idol. "Now run
away, for I must close these papers in time
for Oliver, who rides dispatch to Fort
Trumbull to-night. And, Betty," as she

stood glowing and smiling before him, " my
child, you grow more like your mother every
day," and with a hasty movement General
Wolcott turned away to conceal his emotion, as Betty went quickly from the room.

CHAPTER VI

It had been a wild night, and the morning wind sobbed and sighed through the elms, which, denuded of their leaves, stood out tall and bare against the leaden sky, and there was a chill in the air that might betoken snow. Pamela Wolcott stood in the sitting-room window and sighed softly, as she gazed out at the November landscape, letting her fingers beat soft tattoo against the lozenge-shaped pane.

"Pamela," said Betty from the depths of a big chair, where she sat busily knitting a little stocking whose proportions suggested Miss Moppet, "I wish you would stop that devil's march. Believe me, you had much better come and talk to me, and so drive away the vapors, rather than stand there and worry over the whereabouts of Josiah."

"It will take more than that to drive away the thoughts I cannot help," said Pamela, coming back from the window and seating herself on the wide settle, for Pamela was somewhat given to seeking the warmest corner, and dreaded a New England winter. "It is full time I had some intelligence, for Josiah promised that he would take advantage of any courier who started for New London to dispatch me a letter, and you know that father had news two days since from Morristown, but nothing came for me. Betty, I am sore afraid of evil tidings."

"You are ever faint-hearted," said Betty, glancing compassionately at her sister.

"And I dreamed last night of a wedding," went on Pamela, "and that, you know, is an evil sign."

"Best not let Aunt Euphemia hear you," replied Betty, with a smile. "You have been consulting Chloe, I am sure, as to the portents of dreams. Fie, Pamela; Josiah is strong and well, and there is not likely to be a movement of the troops just now, father says, so why worry? I am anxious because we hear nothing of Clarissa, and I think Aunt Euphemia is the same, for I heard her talking and sighing last night when Miss Bidwell carried up the night light. Dear Clarissa, how I wish I could see her again; I wonder if she be quite, quite happy shut up in New York among the Tories."

"No doubt; though when she married Gulian Verplanck we had little thought of the occupation of New York by the British. Do you recollect how pretty she looked on her wedding-day, Betty, and the little caps you and I wore, — mine with a knot of blue, and yours of rose-color? I found that ribbon one day last week, tucked away in a little box. Have you kept yours?"

"No," returned Betty, with a sudden blush and a quick, half-guilty throb of her heart, as she remembered in whose hand she had last seen that same bow of rose-color; "that is, I had it until last summer, when — I lost it." And Betty dropped two stitches in her confusion, which fortunately Pamela was too much engrossed in her own thoughts to notice."

"It is five years last May," said Pamela. "You and I were tiny things of ten and eleven years, and Oliver strutted about grand and dignified in a new coat. The first wedding in our family — I wonder whose will be the next?"

"Yours, of course," said Betty quickly. "That is if you and Josiah can ever make up your minds. I will not be like you, Pamela; trust me, when my turn comes I'll know full well whether I will or I won't." And Betty tossed her saucy head with a mischievous laugh as there came a rap on the front door which caused both girls to start up and fly to the window.

"Why, 't is Sally Tracy," cried Betty. "I did not know she had returned from her visit to Lebanon." And she ran rapidly along the hall, and opening the door, embraced her friend with all a girl's enthusiasm.

"Welcome, Sally," said Pamela, as the pair came hand in hand towards her. "Betty has been moping ever since you left, and had a desperate fit of industry from sheer loneliness. I really believe she has made a stocking and a half for Moppet — or was it a pair, Betty?"

"The second pair, if you please," retorted Betty, rejoiced to see Pamela smile, even if at her own expense; "and Miss Bidwell says they are every bit as fine as yours."

"They may well be that," said Pamela, whose pet detestation was the manufacture

of woolen stockings (then considered one of
the component parts of a girl's education in
New England). "But Sally is such a marvelous knitter that she will no doubt rejoice
at your success. Had you as severe weather
in Lebanon as this? I am fearful that we
will have a hard winter, the cold has set in
so early."

"They have had one flurry of snow already," Sally answered, "but not so much
wind as we of Litchfield rejoice in. But I
had a merry visit and saw much company.
Dolly bemoaned daily that you could not
come, Pamela."

"I am to go later, after or about the day
set apart for Thanksgiving. But you and
Betty have much to say to each other, and I
will not interrupt you; Miss Bidwell has
something for me to do, I'll warrant; so,
farewell for the present, Sally." And Pamela left the room.

"Come, sit beside me on the settle," said
Betty, putting Sally in the warmest seat.
"Your fingers are cold, and the room is not
yet sufficiently warm. Well," — with a sig-
nificant smile, — "what have you to tell
me?"

"Not what you think," with a smiling

nod, "for Francis Plunkett is far too pressing for my taste," answered Sally.

"Ha, ha," quoth Betty, much amused,
"is that the way you take it? Then I fore-
see that Francis will win for his much speaking."

"Indeed he will not; I teased him well
the last evening, and he dare not resume
the subject for a while at least."

"Then there is some one else," said Betty.
"Can it be that Oliver" —

"Oh, no," cried Sally hastily; "Oliver
has not such an idea, believe me, Betty."

"How can you answer for him?" retorted
Betty, laughing. "But your tone answers
for yourself, so I must guess again. I think
I have heard something of a handsome
young lawyer from Branford" —

"Fie!" cried Sally, in her turn averting
her face quickly, but not before Betty had
perceived her heightened color. "I have
but met him three times, and there are
plenty of other personable men as well as
he, for while one stops with Dolly the officers from Fort Trumbull are ever coming
and going, you know."

"Ah, Sally, you are growing giddy, I
fear," continued Betty with comical pretense

of solemnity. "I think it behooves me to caution you."

"Caution me, indeed!" laughed Sally. "Wait until we both go, as we all are invited to Hartford with Dolly this winter when the Assembly meets, and then see if you be not fully as giddy as I am."

"I do not believe that I can go to Hartford, Sally; you know Pamela is more Dolly's friend than mine, and I think she needs some diversion, for ever since Josiah had his commission and joined the Continental army, she has nearly moped herself to death. And Pamela is like my mother, not very strong; I can see that Aunt Euphemia is somewhat troubled about her even now, so perhaps our fine schemes for a trip to Hartford may have to be given up, at least so far as my going is concerned."

Sally's face fell; the visit to Hartford had been so long talked of, and Betty's presence so much desired, that this was a dash of the coldest possible water.

"Oh, Betty, how truly sorry I shall be. But let us hope for the best. It will be a sad breaking up of all my plans for the winter if you cannot come. I was also to stop at Fairfield with Mrs. Sherman, but since

the raid of last summer her health has been
so shattered that all thoughts of visitors
have to be abandoned, and therefore I was
counting upon our merry visit to Dolly as
compensation."

Sally looked so melancholy at this point
that Betty took her hand and was about to
take a rather more hopeful view of things,
but the words died on her lips as the clatter
of a horse's feet was heard outside, and both
girls ran to the window in time to see the
rider draw rein at the south door of the
mansion and dismount in apparent haste.

" It is some dispatch," said Betty breathlessly. " Did you not see the bag he carried
at the saddle? And there is my father —
oh, Sally, I wonder if there be news from
General Washington and the army?" and
struck by the sudden fear of ill-tidings the
girls ran hastily from the room.

In the wide hall stood Miss Bidwell, and
beside her the stranger, saddle-bag in hand,
as Miss Euphemia emerged from the dining-
room, whence General Wolcott had preceded
her.

" From the commander-in-chief, general,"
said the courier, touching his battered hat in
salute, " and special dispatches from Gen-

eral Steuben. Also this private packet, which was lying waiting at King's Bridge Inn; I have been four days on the road, owing to my horse having lamed himself when near Chatham, and I could not make time on the nag which stands at your door."

"King's Bridge," murmured Miss Euphemia: "then there is news of Clarissa. Brother, have I your permission?"—as General Wolcott gave the small packet into her hand.

"Break the seals," said the general briefly, "and bring me the letters presently to my study. See that the horse and man be well taken care of: I may have to dispatch instant answer to these," and he went quickly down the hall, closing the door behind him.

With fingers that trembled somewhat, Miss Euphemia opened the cover, and disclosed three letters to the eager eyes of the girls, who stood breathless beside her.

"One for your father (it is Gulian Verplanck's hand), this for me, from Clarissa, and the smaller one for you, Betty; let us go into the sitting-room and read ours together."

"None for me?" said Pamela's despairing voice, with a sob treading on the words ; " oh, I fear me some evil has befallen Josiah."

" No, no," whispered Betty, stealing her hand lovingly into her sister's, as she pulled her gently into the room ; " father has the dispatches ; these are but the long-looked-for letters from New York, Pamela, and I 'll wager there is something from Josiah among father's packets. Let us see what my letter says," and Betty, having seated Pamela and Sally on the settle, placed herself on a convenient cricket, and broke the seal of her letter. But before her eyes had time to see more than " Dearest Betty," she was interrupted by a sudden exclamation from her aunt.

" Clarissa has been at death's door," cried Miss Euphemia, startled out of her usual composure. " I knew this long silence boded no good. Listen, I will read it," and the three girls gathered round her chair at once.

" Dear and Honored Aunt " (ran the letter), " I take up my pen, after many days of pain and dire distress, to send loving greetings to you, my Beloved father, and my dear sisters. For the hand of death was nearly

.upon me : thank God that I am still preserved to my dear Husband and to you.

" It was a very malignant and severe attack of Fever, and Gulian procured the services of no less than three Physicians, as for days I laid unconscious. My little baby died at two hours old, and I never saw him. Alas, how I have suffered ! I am now very weak, altho' able to be dressed and sit up each day. This is my first letter; and I pine so sorely for you, my dear ones, that my dear Husband permits me to write, and begs with me that you will permit one of my sisters to come to me and cheer my heart " —

" Come to her ! Good lack ! " cried impetuous Betty, interrupting the reader, " how is one to go when the British are in occupation ? " —

" How, indeed," sighed Miss Euphemia ; " but perhaps the letter will tell," and she resumed her reading, after wiping her eyes softly. " Where was I ? — oh " —

" Father will no doubt be able to procure a pass from General Washington, which will admit the bearer into the City, and Gulian will himself be ready when you advise us, and will await you at King's Bridge

Inn. Dear Aunt, send me some one soon, and let me see a dear home face, else I shall die of grief and homesickness, far from my own people.

"Your loving and obedient niece,

"CLARISSA VERPLANCK."

By this time Pamela was sobbing aloud, and tears flowed down Miss Euphemia's cheeks, but Betty sprang to her feet with a little impatient stamp, crying, —

"Aunt, aunt, which of us shall go? Pamela, you are a gentle and charming nurse; shall it be you?"

"I!" sighed Pamela; "oh, I would go to the world's end for Clarissa."

"But this is to go to New York," cried Betty, with unconscious irony; "and as we can neither of us go alone, why could not my father arrange for one of us to accompany Mrs. Seymour, who leaves shortly to be near her brother for the winter? Did you not tell me, Sally, that she was going to New York?"

"Yes," answered Sally Tracy, "she has been making all manner of preparations, for, as you know, her brother is imprisoned in the city; and since her acceptance of the

pleasure coach from the Mayor of New York
(which he presented her with when he was
released from Litchfield gaol), she has been
pining to go to him. And, beside, she travels in her coach as far as possible ; and my
mother said last night that General Washington was to send her safe-conduct through
our lines to the city."

" We must first consult your father," said
Miss Euphemia gravely, much upset by the
suggestion of making up her mind to do anything in haste, for she was a very deliberate
person, and despised hurried decisions. " I
will find him as soon as he has finished the
dispatches, and, moreover, this letter to him
from Gulian may have directions. I incline
to think that you, Betty, will be the one to
go. Pamela can scarce bear the journey in
this weather," and gathering her papers
carefully in her hand, Miss Euphemia left
the room, and the girls gazed blankly at
each other with startled eyes and throbbing
hearts.

CHAPTER VII

WHAT FOLLOWED A LETTER

"IT was all decided last night," said Betty, tucking her little feet carefully under her gown and clasping her knees with her hands to keep them warm, as she sat in Moppet's chair, which stood close by the fire, where a log burned and crackled in the big chimney — a most unusual luxury for those days, and granted only to Moppet's youth and slight delicacy of constitution. "Father found the pass from General Washington among his dispatches brought by the courier; and as it includes Mrs. Seymour's maid, he arranged with her that I go instead, as Mrs. Seymour kindly says she can procure another attendant in New York. I can scarce believe it possible, Sally. Oh, fancy my having to live in a city occupied by the British!"

"Ah," sighed Miss Moppet, pressing her head against Betty's knee, and a spark of

interest lighting up her doleful little face,
" if only some of them be like my good " —

" Oh, some of the Tories may be passably
amusing," said Betty hastily, giving Moppet
a warning glance, as she checked the words
on the child's lips by a soft touch of her
hand. " I doubt not that Gulian, my
brother-in-law, has fine qualities, else Clarissa had not been so fond of him as to leave
us all and go so far from us. But I trust
that even Gulian may not see fit to talk
loyalist to me; my naughty tongue would
get me into trouble straightway."

" You must learn to control your tongue,
Betty," said Moppet primly, with a roguish
twinkle of her eyes upward. " Miss Bidwell says mine is an unruly member, and
told me a most dire tale of a little girl whose
mother for punishment pricked her tongue
with a hot bodkin."

" Ugh!" cried Sally, with a shudder, " that
was in Puritan days, truly."

" I do not crave the hot bodkin," said
Betty, laughing. " Miss Bidwell's tales are
a trifle gruesome, Moppet."

" But I always do love a flimming tale,
Betty " (this was Moppet's invariable ren-
dering of the word " thrilling," which her

lips had never yet conquered), "and some of them are most bloody ones, I assure you. Oh, Betty, Betty, what *shall* I do when you are gone!" and with a sudden realization of her loss, Moppet gave a quick sob which went to Betty's heart.

"Nay, sweetheart, be a brave little maid," she answered, fighting a small lump in her own throat. "I would I could take you with me; but as I cannot, you must hasten to learn how to make better pot-hooks and write me letters, which Aunt Euphemia will forward with hers. And, Moppet, I think I shall give you in special charge to Sally; how will that please you?"

"I love Sally," said the child simply, as the tender-hearted Sally knelt down beside her. "Will you help console me with my primer and that altogether dreadful sampler when my Betty is away?"

"Indeed will I," replied Sally, much amused with Moppet's view of the sampler; "and you shall come and see me every fine day, and the wet ones I am sure to be here with Pamela, who has proclaimed her intention of adopting me when Betty goes. And now I must be going, for it is nearly the dinner hour, and my mother says as I have

dined here three days she bespeaks my presence for one out of four. So farewell until
to-morrow, Betty, when I shall be here to
see you start upon your travels."

Betty was busy enough all that day; indeed, nothing more than a confused recollection remained with her afterward of trunk
and two small boxes to be packed; of Pamela's urging her acceptance of a new lute-
string slip, rose-colored, which had recently
come to her from Boston; of Miss Bidwell's
innumerable stockings all tucked carefully
away in one corner of the hair-covered brass-
nailed box, and even Miss Moppet's tenderly
cherished blue bag embroidered in steel
beads, which had belonged to their mother,
but which Moppet insisted could be used by
Betty with great effect for her handkerchief
at a ball.

" Ball, indeed," sighed Betty, whose brave
heart was beginning to quail at thought of
an untold length of separation from her
beloved family. " I should think the hearts
of the patriots imprisoned in New York
would scarce be occupied with balls in such
times as these."

"You mistake," said Pamela, who, truth
to tell, half longed for Betty's opportunities,

for was not her sister going somewhere near
Josiah's post? "I am sure Clarissa's letter
which you read me bade you bring all your
best gowns and finery, and we have all
heard how gay the army of occupation make
the city."

"Aye, to those who are Tories," said
Betty, with curling red lips, "but for me —
oh, Miss Bidwell, if you put in another pair
of stockings I shall require as many feet as
a centipede, who I read has hundreds of
them."

"Hundreds of feet?" echoed Miss Moppet. "Oh, Betty, do I live to hear you tell
a fairy tale as if it were real?"

"Read your primer, and you will learn
many wonderful things," quoth Betty,
snatching up the child in her arms. "I
shall take you straightway to bed, for we
must be up betimes in the morning, you
know."

Very carefully and tenderly did Betty
bathe Moppet's sweet little face, comb and
smooth the pretty curling hair, so like her
own save in color, and then run the brass
warming-pan, heated by live coals, through
the sheets lest her tender body suffer even a
slight chill. And when Moppet was safely

lodged in bed Betty sat down beside her to
hold her hand until she dropped asleep.
But between excitement and grief the child's
eyes would not close, and she asked question
after question, until Betty finally announced
she should answer no more.

Moppet lay still for some moments, and
just as Betty was beginning to fancy that
the long, dark eyelashes were curling downward in sleepy comfort the dark blue eyes
opened, and a dancing imp of mischief
gleamed from their depths in Betty's face.

" When you meet Captain Yorke, Betty,"
whispered Moppet, " be sure you tell him
how Oliver and Josiah hunted and hunted
that morning, and how I never, never
told " —

"Moppet," said Betty, turning a vivid
pink in the firelight, " how can you ! " —

" Yes," pursued Moppet relentlessly, "and
you give him my love — heaps of it — and I
just hope he may never get taken a prisoner
during the whole war again."

" Go to sleep, dear," answered Betty, biting her lip ; but her cheeks did not grow
cool until long after the soft, regular breath-
ing told that her little sister had gone into
the land of dreams.

The Wolcott household was up early that
cold winter morning, when Mrs. Seymour's
coach, with its pair of sturdy, strong gray
horses, drew up at the front door. It took
some twenty minutes to bestow Betty's trunk
and boxes on the rumble behind, during
which time Mrs. Seymour alighted and received all manner of charges and advice
from Miss Euphemia, who, now that Betty
was fairly on the wing, felt much sinking of
heart over her departure. Mrs. Seymour,
a pretty young matron, whose natural gayety
of spirit was only subdued by the anxiety
she was suffering in regard to her only
brother, now a prisoner in New York (and
for whose exchange she was bringing great
influence to bear in all directions), listened
with much outward deference and inward
impatience to the stately dame, and turned
with an air of relief to General Wolcott
when he announced that all was ready for
their departure, and with much courtliness
offered his hand to conduct her to her
coach.

"That you will take the best care of my
daughter I am assured, madam," said the
gallant gentleman. "It is our great good
fortune to have found this opportunity and

your kind escort, for owing to the shortness
of time I have not been able to notify my
son-in-law of Betty's coming. But as you
are going into the city yourself, I depend
upon you to keep her with you until you
can place her safely in Gulian Verplanck's
hands. I trust that you have General
Washington's pass close by you? It is
quite possible that you may need it even
before you reach White Plains; there are
many marauding parties who infest the
country beyond us."

"It is here, general," replied Mrs. Seymour, touching the breast of her gown. "I
thought it well to carry it about my person,
as I am told that even the Hessians respect
General Washington's safe-conduct to enter
New York."

Betty, with crimson cheeks, but brave
smiling eyes, threw her arms fondly around
Miss Euphemia, Pamela, Sally, and Miss
Bidwell, all in turn, but Moppet's soft cry
as she buried her face in her hands made
her lip quiver, and as she bent her head for
her father's farewell, a reluctant tear forced
itself down her cheek.

"The God of our fathers be with you, my
daughter," he said, taking her in his arms;

" my love and blessing to Clarissa and her
husband. Remain with them until I find
safe opportunity to have you return to us ;
advise us often of your health and, I trust,
continued well-being ; keep a brave heart as
befits your name and lineage ; fare you well,
fare you well ! "

Betty sank back trembling into her seat
beside Mrs. Seymour, the door was closed,
and as the coach rolled off she caught a
parting glimpse of Miss Moppet lifted high
in General Wolcott's arms, kissing her hand
fondly as she waved good-by.

"DRAT that knocker!" said Peter Provoost.

The house stood on Wall Street, and to the fact that it like a few others had been built of brick, it owed its escape from the fire which ravaged the city in 1776, the fire which also destroyed old Trinity Church, leaving the unsightly ruin standing for some years in what was aristocratic New York of the period. It was a square, comfortable-looking mansion, with the Dutch *stoep* in front, and the half-arch of small-paned glass above the front door, which was painted white and bore a massive brass knocker. That same knocker was a source of much irritation to Peter Provoost; for although he was of fair size for his thirteen years, he could barely reach it when mounted on the very tips of his toes, and even then never dared touch its shining surface unless his fingers were clean — a desirable state of

neatness which, alas! did not often adorn the
luckless Peter. For though tidy and careful enough when appearing before his guar-
dians, Mr. and Mrs. Verplanck, it must be
confessed that going to and from school
Peter was prone to lay down both books and
hat, oftentimes in the mud, and square himself pugnaciously if he chanced to meet one
of the boys of the " Vly Market," who were
wont to scoff and tease the Broadway boys
unmercifully; and fierce battles were the
frequent outcome of the feeling between the
two sections, and in those Peter invariably
took part.

The family was a small one, and consisted
of Gulian Verplanck and his wife, his
grandmother, Mrs. Effingham, a lovely old
Quakeress, and Peter, who, having lost both
parents at an early age, had remained in
Albany with his other guardian, Mr. Abram
Lansing, until some six months before,
when it was decided that he should go to
New York and be under the Verplanck
eye; and although Peter had rebelled much
against the plan in the first place, he found
himself much happier under Clarissa's gentle
rule, and positively adored her in conse-
quence. The only lion in Peter's path at

present was the strong Tory proclivity of the head of the house; and although he had been warned by his Albany friends to be prudent and respectful, the boy had inherited a sturdy patriotism which burned all the more hotly for its repression.

On this cold December afternoon Peter stood, books in hand, and surveyed that aggravating knocker from his stand on the sidewalk. He was painfully conscious that his feet were muddy, and his chubby fingers certainly needed soap and water; it was Friday, and Pompey, one of the black servants, had evidently been scrubbing the front steps. Therefore Peter debated whether it would be wiser to skirt around the mansion and gain entrance by the area steps, where no doubt he would encounter Dinah, the cook (who objected to invasions of unclean shoes), or boldly ascend the front steps, struggle with that balefully glittering knocker, and trust to Pompey's somewhat dim eyes to escape remonstrance before he could gain his own room and make himself presentable. The chances of a scolding seemed pretty equally balanced to Peter, and he heaved a deep sigh and put his foot on the first immaculate step before him as a hand fell on his shoulder and a merry voice said behind him : —

"What in the world are you pondering, Peter? I have watched you since I turned the corner of Broadway, and truly for once have seen you stand absolutely still. In some scrape with the Vly boys, I'll warrant; do you wish me to come in and plead for you?" and Kitty Cruger tripped lightly up the steps as she beckoned Peter to follow.

"Now you have done it — not I!" said Peter, with a mischievous chuckle, as he tore up after her.

"Done what?" asked mystified Kitty. She and Peter were fast friends.

"Muddied the clean steps," quoth Peter with gleeful brevity.

"Have I?" glancing down carelessly until she saw each dainty footprint plainly depicted on the white marble, side by side with Peter's heavier tracks. "Oh, what a shame," reaching up successfully to the brass knocker; "but I am sure Pompey will forgive me, and you can" — stopping short as the door opened and Pompey himself stood bowing low in the hall.

"Good-day, missy," said he, for Kitty Cruger was a frequent and welcome visitor at the Verplancks'. "Miss Clarissa is pretty well to-day, thank you, and ole madam is in the drawing-room — Law!" catching sight of Peter, who was skillfully slipping down the hall in Kitty's wake. "Dat you, Massa Peter? Reckon you better hurry, for it's mos' time for dinner, sah."

But Peter, with great discretion, paused not for reply as he vanished up a back staircase and reached his own chamber, panting but triumphant.

"Good-day, dear grandma," said Kitty, crossing the hall as Pompey held open the door of the drawing-room; "I was detained by reason of the sewing-bee at the Morrises', and have barely time to see you and ask for Clarissa."

"How does thee do?" said Grandma Effingham, drawing her little drab shawl more closely around her shapely shoulders as she laid down her knitting. "I am pleased to see thee. Clarissa is somewhat stronger to-day; thee knows she has been more like her old self since Gulian dispatched the letters asking that one of her sisters be allowed to come to her. The poor child pines for a home face; it is natural; thee sees she has been long absent from her people."

"Surely it is almost time to get some reply," said Kitty, as she kissed the dear old Quakeress, for Kitty was one of Mrs. Effingham's grandchildren, although her mother had been read out of meeting for having married one of the "world's people." "I doubt that Clarissa will shortly begin to worry and grow ill again unless kind Providence sends some tidings."

"Nay, nay," said grandma gently. "If thee had half Clarissa's patience it would be thy gain, Kitty."

Grandma was such a quaint, pretty picture, as she sat in her straight-backed chair, with her Quaker cap and steel-gray silk gown, her sleeves elbow-cut, displaying still plump and rounded arms (although she was nearly seventy), and her smooth white fingers flew rapidly in and out of the blue yarn as she resumed her knitting of Peter's stocking. Peter was rather a godsend to grandma in the matter of stockings; no wool that was ever carded could resist his vigorous onslaughts, and it kept grandma busy all her spare moments to supply his restless feet with warm covering.

"Patience," echoed Kitty, with a comical sigh. "Nay, grandma, give me a few more years without it."

"Fie," said grandma, gazing at the bright
face with her indulgent eye; "eighteen is
full late to begin to learn to conform to thy
elders. I was married and the twins were
born at thy age, Kitty."

"Good lack," quoth Kitty. "Where are
the men nowadays, grandma? Save for
the redcoats, and I am not so daft over Sir
Henry Clinton's gay officers as some — no
doubt 't is my Quaker blood — except for
the officers, where are our gallants? Some
of mine are up the Hudson beyond the neutral ground, others with the rebels at Morristown."

"Hush," said grandma, with an uneasy
glance toward the door; "do not talk of
rebels in this house: had n't thee better run
up and see Clarissa?"

"If Miss Kitty pleases," spoke the voice
of Pompey at the door, "will she walk upstairs? Young madam wants to see her."

"Coming," said Kitty, kissing grandma
fondly, and then following Pompey as he
marched gravely up to open the door of
Mrs. Verplanck's morning-room. It was a
tiny apartment: for when Gulian Verplanck
brought his young bride home he had added
a room to the wing below, and as it greatly

enlarged their bedroom, the happy idea had
struck him to throw up a partition, corner-
ways, which formed an irregularly shaped
room opening on the passage, and gave
Clarissa her own cherished den in that great
house of square rooms and high ceilings.
In it she had placed all her home belong-
ings; her spinnet, which had been her
mother's (brought by sloop to New York
from New Haven), found the largest space
there, and her grandmother's small spinning-
wheel was in the corner near the chimney-
piece which Gulian had contrived to have
put in lest his delicate wife might suffer
with cold.

Near the small log which blazed brightly
on the hearth, in a low chair made somewhat easy with cushions, sat a fair, fragile-
looking, girlish figure, in whose mournful
dark eyes was something so pathetic that it
suggested the old-time prophecy that such
"die young." Clarissa Verplanck in that
resembled none of her family, and the one
reason for her father's and aunt's anxiety
about her was that she was thought the
image of a sister of her mother who fulfilled
the prophecy. Be that as it may, Clarissa
was anything but a mournful person in gen-

eral; her spirits were somewhat prone to
outrun her physical strength, and therefore
her sad little appeal for one of her sisters to
cheer her had come in the light of a demand
to the Litchfield home, and alarmed them
more than anything else could have done.

" Kitty, Kitty," said Clarissa, holding out
a welcoming hand to her visitor, who seated
herself on a cricket beside her, " why have
you not been in this four days ? I am truly
glad to see you, for ever since Gulian and I
dispatched our letters to my father I have
been so cross and impatient that I fear my
good husband is beginning to tire of his
bargain, and lament a peevish wife."

" Heaven forgive you for the slander,"
retorted Kitty, laughing ; " if ever there
was a husband who adored the ground you
walk on, Gulian is " —

" Thank you," said a quiet voice, as a tall
dark man entered from the bedroom.

" Let me finish my sentence — Gulian is
that benighted swain," burst in Kitty.

" Again, my thanks," answered Gulian
gravely. To none but Clarissa was he ever
seen to relax his serious manner ; perhaps
hers were the only eyes who saw the tender-
ness behind the stern, reserved exterior.

He really liked his cousin; but although Kitty was not, like most people, afraid of him, it must be confessed that he wearied her, and she much preferred to have her gossip with Clarissa when Gulian was safely out of the house.

"And now tell me about the letters," pursued Kitty. "You sent for your sister, grandma told me. Which one, Clarissa?"

"Indeed, I do not know; I left the choice to my father, but I think — I hope it may be Betty. I only wish I might have Moppet as well," and the quickly checked sigh told Gulian's keen ears what the unuttered thought had been.

"Betty — let me see — is that the sister next yourself?"

"Oh, no; the sister next to me in age died in infancy. Then comes Oliver, and then Pamela, who is seventeen now, and next my Betty. How I wonder if the girls have changed; five years makes a long gap, you know, and even my imagination can scarce fill it. Do you fancy we will hear soon, Gulian?"

"I cannot tell," he said gently, thinking how often he had sought reply to the same question in the past week, and longing tenderly to give her the expected pleasure.

"It may be that General Wolcott may find some chance opportunity to send his daughter at once, in which event you know there would scarce be time to hear before she would reach us."

"Oh, Gulian," cried Clarissa, clasping her hands, as a faint pink glow lit her pale face, "you did not say that before. If it were only possible " —

"Why not?" said Kitty encouragingly.

"But, Gulian, you said in the letter that you would await my sister at King's Bridge Inn. Surely you cannot go there and stop, waiting at the Inn for days?"

"I can ride out to-morrow, and, in fact, I hastened through some business at the wharf to-day which enabled me to have the day free. I can easily go to King's Bridge and inquire at the Inn for dispatches; you will not mind my being absent all day? Perhaps Kitty will come and bear you company while I am gone?"

"Right gladly," replied Kitty; "will you ride alone, Gulian?"

"I might, easily," said Gulian; "but when I procured a pass from Sir Henry Clinton yesterday (it is an eight days' pass, Clarissa) I found that Captain Yorke goes to-morrow to the neutral ground to inspect troops, and I think I shall take advantage of his company."

" I am glad of that," said Clarissa, putting her slender hand in Gulian's and looking with grateful eyes up at him, as he stood beside her chair. " Is he the aide-de-camp you told me of, Gulian, for whom you had taken a liking ? "

" The same : a fine, manly fellow, the second son of Lord Herbert Yorke, one of my father's old friends in England. You were dancing with him at the De Lanceys' ' small and early,' were you not, Kitty, last week ? "

" Yes," said Kitty, with a quick nod and a half frown, " he has the usual airs and graces of a newly arrived officer from the mother-country."

" Perhaps you find the colonists more to your mind," responded Gulian somewhat severely ; but Clarissa gave his sleeve a warning twitch, as Kitty made answer with heightened color : —

" My own countrymen are ever first with me, as you know full well, Gulian, but one must dance sometimes to keep up one's heart in these times, and Captain Yorke has a passably good step which suits with mine."

What Gulian would have replied to this was never known, for at that moment an outcry arose in the hall, followed by the bump, bump of some heavy body rolling down the staircase, and Peter's boyish voice shouting out, between gasps of laughter, —

"Pompey, Pompey, I say! — it's nobody but me: oh, what a proper old goose it is; do, somebody come and thrash him."

In a second Gulian and Kitty were outside the door, and beheld at the foot of the winding stairs poor Pompey, picking himself up, with many groans and much rubbing of his shins, while Peter, rolling himself nearly double with laughter, stood midway of the flight, with a queer object in his hand which Gulian seized hastily.

"It's only a gourd," gasped Peter between paroxysms. "I kept it in my closet for a week, and half an hour ago I stole a bit of wick out of Dinah's pantry and dipped it well in melted tallow, and then stuck it inside, when, as you see, having carved out two eyes and a slit for the nose, it looks somewhat ghastly when the light comes forth."

"It's a debbil, debbil," cried Pompey. "Massa Peter sent me to find his skates,

and dat awful face " — Pompey's teeth chat-
tered, and Peter went off in a fresh burst
of laughter.

" It scared him properly, Uncle Gulian;
and though I ran after him and shook it
(it only looks gruesome in the dark, you
know) he never stopped, and he stumbled
on the first step, and then he rolled — My!
how he did bump " — and naughty Peter
sat down on the stairs and held his sides for
very merriment.

" You ought to be ashamed of yourself,"
said Gulian sternly, to whom practical jokes
were an utter abomination, " and you deserve to be well punished. Pompey, stop
groaning, and inform me at once whether
you have sustained any injury by your fall."

" Law, Massa Gulian, you tink falling
down dat stair gwine to hurt dis chile ? "
began Pompey, who entertained a warm
affection for the mischievous Peter and
dreaded nothing so much as a scolding
from his master. " Dose stairs don't 'mount
to nuffin ; ef it had been de area steps dey
moughten be dangerous. Massa knows
boys mus' have dey fun ; please 'cuse me
for makin' such a bobbery."

" Well, I did it," said Peter sturdily, in-

stantly sobered by the expression of his
uncle's face, and his generous heart touched
with Pompey's defense of his prank, "and
nobody helped me, so let's have the whip-
ping right off before dinner, please, Uncle
Gulian, and then I can eat in peace —
even if I am a trifle sore," wound up the
sinner ruefully.

Gulian Verplanck's sense of humor was
not keen, but the situation was too much
for him, and a queer, grim smile lit up his
eyes, as he said slowly : —

" As Pompey seems more frightened than
hurt, and has interceded for you, I shall
not punish you this time, Peter ; but recollect that the very first occasion after this
that you see fit to practice a joke on any
member of my household, your skates will
be confiscated for the remainder of the
winter," and with a warning glance he followed Kitty back into his wife's room, leaving Pompey on the staircase, still rubbing
his bruised shins, while the irrepressible
Peter indulged once more in a convulsion
of silent laughter which bent him double
and threatened to burst every button off his
tightly fitting jacket.

CHAPTER IX

MRS. SEYMOUR, having had the advantage of some weeks to form her plans, had carefully arranged everything for her own comfort, so far as was possible, and Betty Wolcott, after the first pang of parting was over, began to enjoy the novelty of the journey most thoroughly. Except for a few days spent at Lebanon, Betty had never been from home in her life, and being, as we have seen, a bit of a philosopher in her own quaint fashion, after the first day spent in Mrs. Seymour's cheerful society she found herself much less homesick than she had expected. To begin with, the coach was, for those times, very comfortable. It was English-built, and had been provided with capacious pockets in unexpected places; it amused Betty exceedingly to find that she was seated over the turkey, ham, cake, and even a goodly pat of butter, carefully packed in a small stone jar, while another compartment held several changes of linen, powder, a small mirror, a rouge pot, and some brushes. Mrs. Seymour had been born and bred in New York, and many of her people were Tories; therefore she hoped to assist the brother who, breaking apart from the others, had taken up arms for the colonists.

Cæsar, Mrs. Seymour's coachman, was a colored man of middle age, a slave of her father's, and, having been brought from New York to Connecticut, knew the route fairly well. They broke the journey first at a small roadside tavern, where the horses were baited, while Betty and Mrs. Seymour gladly descended, and warmed themselves well by the kitchen fire, taking a drink of warm milk, for which the good woman who had invited them inside refused payment. She was deeply interested when Mrs. Seymour told her of their errand, and followed them out to the door of the coach, bringing with her own hands the soapstone which she had carefully warmed for their feet, and she waved a kindly good-by as they rode off, delighted at seeing, for the first time in her life, a " pleasure coach."

The first night was spent by the travelers in Danbury, where they proceeded to the

house of Mrs. Seymour's cousin, Mrs. Beebe,
and were most warmly welcomed. The
Beebe household, which consisted of Mrs.
Beebe and seven children (Captain Beebe
being with the Connecticut Rangers),
trooped out, one and all, to meet them, to
inspect the coach, interview Cæsar, and admire the horses.   Billy, the second boy, fra-
ternized with Betty at once : and after
learning all the mysteries of the coach pockets, helping Cæsar to unharness, and superintending the fetching of an extra large log
for the fireplace, he roasted chestnuts in the
ashes as they sat around the chimney-piece,
and told Betty thrilling stories of the attack
on Danbury by the British.

"We dragged the feather-beds up to the
window," said Billy, "and mother stuffed a
pillow or two in the cracks.   My, how the
bullets did fly !   The children were all bid
to stay in the attic ; but as the roof shelves,
you know, it became pretty hot, especially
when the fires began, and then mother did
get frightened, more especially when she saw
the blaze of the Woolford house, down the
street.   Did n't I just wish I was a man, to
go and help father that day !   Luckily for
us, the wind was in the other direction ;
father said that was all that saved us."

" And Divine Providence, my son," said Mrs. Beebe's soft voice, as she laid a hand on the boy's shoulder. "Billy's only experience of war was a sharp one for a few hours. He has been longing ever since to join his father, but I can only find it in my mother's heart to rejoice that he is too young to do so. Now, Billy, light the candles; for if our friends must resume their journey tomorrow, it is full time to retire."

Betty found the little room assigned to her, with Billy's assistance, but before he left her he pointed out two small holes near the window frame, where bullets had entered and remained buried in the woodwork; and as Betty curled herself up in the centre of the great feather-bed, she thought, with a throb of her girlish heart, that perhaps she, too, might see some of the terrors of war before she returned to the shelter of her dear Litchfield home.

The next morning dawned cold and chilly; a few flakes of snow floated through the air, and Mrs. Beebe urged strongly the wisdom of lying over for twenty-four hours, lest a storm should come and render the roads impassable. But Mrs. Seymour, after a consultation with Cæsar, decided that it was best to push on ; winter was approaching, and each day made the journey less feasible.   There was a fairly good road between them and White Plains, and now that she had started she was impatient to reach the city.   Betty, too, was eager to be off, so with many warm thanks, they again packed the coach and said farewell to the hospitable Beebes, who had insisted on adding fresh stores of provisions to their hamper ; and Billy's last act of friendliness was to slip into Betty's hand a package of taffy, of his own manufacture, which he assured her " was not over-sticky, provided you use care in biting it."

This part of the journey was cold and cheerless enough.   The road wound somewhat, and the settlements were few, even the houses were far apart from each other ; and although the hills were fewer, they heard Cæsar admonish his horses more frequently than usual, and about four o'clock in the day they came to a full stop.   The snow of the morning had turned into a sort of drizzling rain ; and Cæsar, dismounting from his seat, announced to his mistress that one of the horses had cast a shoe.

" What shall we do ? " cried Mrs. Seymour in dismay, preparing to jump down into the mud and investigate matters.

"Dey's no use at all of madam's gettin' out," said Cæsar, holding the door of the coach, — "no use at all. I 'se done got de shoe, 'cause I saw it a-comin' off, an' here it is. De horse will do well enuf, 'caise I 'll drive wif care; but what I wants to say is that, 'cordin' to my jedgment, we had oughter take a turn to de right, just hyar, which am in de direction ob Ridgefield, whar I ken fin' a blacksmith's shop, shuh. Ef madam pleases, it 's goin' somewhat out of de direct way to White Plains, but what wid de weather, which madam can see is obstreperous an' onsartain, I 'm ob de opinion dat Ridgefield am de best stoppin' place for dis night, anyhow;" and having delivered himself of this exhortation, Cæsar touched his hat respectfully, but with an air of having settled the question.

"Very well," said Mrs. Seymour, for she knew Cæsar and Cæsar's ways, and moreover had much confidence in his ability to take care of her, as well as of his horses. "Then take the turn to the right, as you propose. Are you quite sure you are familiar with the road here, Cæsar? It will be dark

soon, and I confess I should not like to lose
our way."

"Not gwine to lose de road wid dis chile
on de box," said Cæsar with fine disdain,
as he climbed to his seat and rolled himself
up warmly again, his teeth chattering as he
did so. But he said to himself, as the
horses started slowly, "Pray de Lord I
ain't mistooken; don't want to fall into none
ob dem old redcoats' han's, Cæsar don't,
dat 's sartain."

Inside the coach, which lumbered on so
slowly that it almost seemed to crawl, Mrs.
Seymour and Betty tried to keep up their
spirits by an occasional remark of cheerful
character, and Betty suggested that perhaps
some bread and cheese from the Beebe
larder would prove satisfactory to Cæsar;
but on asking the question Cæsar only shook
his head, and responded that he was too
busy looking after the horses to eat; and
the long hours dragged on as it grew darker
and darker. Betty rested her head against
the door and peered out at the dripping
trees, whose bare limbs stood like skele-
tons against the leaden sky. Mrs. Seymour
had sunk into a fitful doze by her side.
Suddenly the off horse gave a plunge, the

coach tilted far to one side, and then righted
itself as Cæsar's loud " Whoa, dar ! Steady !
steady ! " was heard. Then Betty saw half a
dozen shadowy forms surround them, and
a voice said sharply, " Who goes there ?
Halt ! " and a hand was laid roughly on the
door of the coach.

" Pray who are you who detain ladies on
a journey ? " said Mrs. Seymour, addressing
the man nearest her. " I am in my own
coach with a maid on our way to New York,
and one of my horses has cast a shoe."

" Stand aside there," said another voice
impatiently, as an officer dismounted from
his horse, and flung the rein to one of the
men. " If you are bound to a city occupied
by the British, you must have safe-conduct,
madam, else we are compelled to search and
detain you."

For answer, Mrs. Seymour drew out a
folded paper, which the officer, straining his
eyes in the fast-fading daylight, read aloud,
as follows : —

" After the expiration of eight days from
the date hereof, Mrs. Seymour and maid
have permission to go into the city of New
York and to return again.

"Given at Morristown this second day of December.

"G. WASHINGTON."

"From the commander-in-chief," said the officer, raising his hat, as he motioned his men to stand back. "Madam, permit me to present myself as Lieutenant Hillhouse of the Connecticut Rangers, and pray command my services."

"Oh," gasped Betty, from the other side, "our own troops. thank Heaven!"

"Truly you are a welcome arrival," said Mrs. Seymour, with a light-hearted laugh. "Betty and I have passed a bad five minutes, fancying you were Hessians. I am on my way to the city to intercede for my brother, Captain Seymour's exchange, and, for the once, I do not mind telling you that my companion is Mistress Betty Wolcott, consigned to my care by her father, General Wolcott, as her sister, Mrs. Verplanck, lies ill in New York, and she goes there to see her, but she travels as my maid."

"I met Lieutenant Hillhouse last summer at my father's house," said Betty, as the young officer came around to her side of the coach, "and right glad I am to see you

now, sir, instead of the redcoats whom
Cæsar, our coachman, has been imagining
would start from every bush as we near
White Plains."

" You are not above a mile from a little
settlement called Ridgefield," answered the
officer; "and while there is no tavern there,
my men and I found fairly comfortable
quarters to-day. If I may suggest, you
should get there as soon as may be."

" We would be glad to," said Mrs. Seymour ruefully, " but one of my horses has
cast a shoe, hence our slow progress. I am
more than glad my servant has not mistaken
the way."

" Madam oughter to know Cæsar better,"
grumbled that worthy from the box.

" How long will it take you to drive the
remaining mile?" said his mistress sooth-
ingly. " We may perhaps have your escort, lieutenant?"

" I am on my return there, madam;
permit me to send my men in advance to
arrange for your comfort, and I will with
pleasure ride beside you until we arrive.
Ridgefield lies beyond that turn," raising
his whip to direct Cæsar. " If it were not
for the growing darkness, you would see the

smoke from the chimney of the house where
I am quartered;" and closing the door of
the coach, the officer gave directions to his
men, who marched quickly down the road,
as he mounted and pursued his way with
the ladies.

Just beyond the farmhouse which Lieutenant Hillhouse had pointed out as his
temporary quarters stood a low, wooden
structure, with a lean-to in the rear, and
there Cæsar drew up his tired horses. A
rather cross-looking spinster stood in the
door of the house, and as Betty and Mrs.
Seymour alighted she said snappishly : —

"I don't own much room, as I told your
men, Mister Lieutenant, but so long as
you 're not Hessians I 'm willing to open
my door for you. It won't be for long, will
it?"

"Oh, no," replied Mrs. Seymour, with her
pretty, gracious smile, "we are simply in
need of a night's lodging. I think we have
food enough in our hampers, and if you can
give us hot milk I have coffee ready for
making."

"I don't begrudge you nothing," said the
woman in a softened tone, as Betty bade
her a pleasant good-day, "but it's a poor

place, anyhow," gazing up at the bare
rafters, " and as I live here all alone I have
to be precious careful of my few things."

" But it 's so neat and clean," said Betty,
pulling a three-legged stool toward the fire,
and surveying the recently scrubbed floor;
" we are cold and weary, and you are very
good to take us in."

Evidently the woman was amenable to
politeness, for she bustled around and insisted upon making the coffee, which Cæsar
produced in due time from his hamper under
the box-seat, and she laid a cloth on the
pine-wood table, and at last, after disappear-
ing for a few minutes into the darkness of
a small inner room, reappeared with three
silver spoons and two forks in her hand,
which she laid carefully down beside the
pewter plates on the table with an air of
pride as she remarked, addressing no one
in particular : —

" The forks was my grandmother's, and
my father fetched the spoons from a voyage
he made on the Spanish main, and he always said they was made of real Spanish
dollars."

Thereupon Mrs. Seymour and Betty
fell to admiring the queer - looking articles

(which from their workmanship) were really
worthy of admiration), and the spinster re-
laxed her severe air sufficiently to accept
a cup of the coffee they were drinking.
And then Mrs. Seymour induced her to give
consent that Cæsar should have a shake-
down in a corner of the kitchen, and although the bed which Betty and the pretty
matron had to share was hard, it was clean,
and the pillows soft, and they slept soundly
and well amid their rough surroundings,
and, to confess the truth, enjoyed the
novelty of the situation.

Lieutenant Hillhouse aroused them early
in the morning by a message; and as Mrs.
Seymour was not ready to receive him,
Betty ran out and met him at the door.

"You look so fresh and bright that I am
sure your night spent upon the roadside
has not harmed you," said the officer, bidding her good-morning. "I am off at once,
as I carry an order to General Wolcott for
quartermaster's stores in Litchfield. What
shall I say to your father for you?"

"Oh," cried Betty, rejoiced at this chance
to send word of mouth to her beloved ones,
"how truly fortunate! Tell my father
we are well and in good spirits, and hope

to reach the neutral ground to-night at farthest."

"You may easily do that; the storm has passed, as you see, and if my friend Caesar can urge his horses somewhat, you are not likely to meet with detentions. One of my men has assisted in shoeing the horse, and if you can, you should start at once."

The coach and Mrs. Seymour appeared at this moment simultaneously, and the lieutenant insisted upon seeing the ladies safely started. Betty seized the opportunity to ask for news of Josiah Huntington, and was told of his having rendered good service, and that he gained in popularity daily.

"And Oliver — my brother," said Betty, leaning from the coach as they were about to move off; "what tidings of him?"

"He has not been with me," replied Hillhouse with some constraint; "indeed, I think he was to be sent on some special service."

"Give him my best affection," said Betty. "And oh, sir, to my little sister at home pray deliver my fondest love," and tears were brimming in Betty's eyes as Caesar flicked his whip at the horses' heads and the coach started.

The road being somewhat better than
that already traveled, the miles which inter-
vened between Ridgefield and White Plains
were more briskly done, and Cæsar had the
satisfaction of pulling up his horses in good
condition before the well-known tavern at
the latter place in time for dinner. The
somewhat pretentious sign hanging out over
the door had been changed to suit the times
and the tempers of the guests, for what had
previously read " The King's Arms, Accom-
modations for Man and Beast," was now
" The Washington Inn," and beneath it a
picture in Continental uniform of a man
whose rubicund countenance required con-
siderable imagination to transform into a
likeness of the commander-in-chief. As
there happened to be a lack of hostlers, it
took some time to get the horses baited, and
it was later than Mrs. Seymour could have
wished when Cæsar finally made his appearance and informed his mistress that all was
ready for their departure. The weather
had been growing colder steadily, and
greatly to their surprise the travelers
learned that in all probability Harlem River
was frozen, and grave doubts were ex-
pressed by mine host of the inn whether

the ladies could gain their journey's end without much discomfort and exposure. But Mrs. Seymour and Betty were both of the opinion that it was inexpedient to linger longer on the road, so for the fourth time they climbed into the coach, and, muffling themselves as closely as possible to keep out the cold, pursued their onward way.

Five miles, eight miles, were covered with fair speed, and Betty's spirits were rising rapidly at the thought that New York and Clarissa were not far away, when Cæsar turned around on his box, and, bringing his horses to a walk, said in an awestruck whisper, —

" 'Fore de Lord, madam, I done suspect de redcoats is comin' ; d' ye heah 'em from de woods ober dar?" pointing with trembling hand in the direction of a sound which rang out on the frosty air at first indistinctly, and then resolved itself into a song.

> " Under the trees in sunny weather,
> Just try a cup of ale together.
> And if in tempest or in storm,
> A couple then, to make you warm,"[1] —

sang a rollicking voice, in fairly good time

---

[1] A topical song then in vogue in New York. (See *Story of the City of New York.*)

and tune, as a group of men came in sight.
As they neared the coach, the man in advance trolled out in an accent which betrayed
his Teutonic origin, —

> "But if the day be very cold,
> Then take a mug of twelve months old!"

" Hello, halt there! " came the command,
as the singer seized the horse by the bridle,
and another soldier dragged Cæsar roughly
from his seat; " who are you, and whence
bound ? "

" Ask my mistress," gasped Cæsar, almost convinced that his last hour had come,
but still having firm faith in Mrs. Seymour.
" Dun you know how to speak to a lady ? "

" I have safe-conduct from General Washington to enter New York," said Mrs. Seymour calmly, extending her hand with the
precious paper toward the first speaker. The
man took it, and gazed stupidly at it. Evidently being German, he could not read it ;
but having turned it upside down and gazed
at it for some seconds, he gave a drunken
leer as he peered inside the coach.

" What you got in your hamper ? blenty
cognac, eh ? Give us a pottle ; that's better
than mugs of ale, eh, poys ? " and he laughed
uproariously.

"I shall give you nothing," said Mrs. Seymour firmly; "if you cannot read my safe-conduct yourself, is there not one of your men who can?"

The Hessian was about to make angry reply, when a young fellow, evidently an Englishman, shoved his way through the men to the coach door.

"Stop that, Joris," he said, prodding the corporal with his elbow; "give me the paper; I can read it." But Joris, who evidently had reached the stage of ugly intoxication, did not choose to give it up, and stood his ground.

"Ve wants cognac," he shouted, "an' you comes out, lady, an' ve'll find for ourselves vhat you is," and seizing Mrs. Seymour by the arm he attempted to drag her from her seat with some violence.

"The pistol, Betty!" cried the plucky little woman as her feet touched the ground; but as Betty, with equally reckless courage, drew their only weapon from its hiding-place, the young Englishman rushed at Joris with an oath, exclaiming, —

"Look out, you fool — here comes the officer's patrol," and there was a clatter of horses' feet, a swift rush, and a voice de-

manding in stern fashion, "Stand back,
there! Whose coach is this? What do you
mean, fellow, by handling a lady in that
manner?" and Geoffrey Yorke struck Joris
a blow with his sheathed sword which nearly
sobered him on the spot.

Back into the corner of the coach sank
Betty, and as she pulled her hood still farther over her face, she felt as if every drop
of blood she possessed was tingling in her
cheeks, as she saw Geoffrey, hat in hand,
dismount and read General Washington's
safe-conduct.

"I deeply regret, madam," he said, with
stately courtesy to Mrs. Seymour, "that a
corporal's guard should have caused you
such annoyance, and I shall see that the fellow who treated you so roughly be properly
punished. Meantime, if you intend to enter
New York you will be obliged to leave your
coach a mile farther on, and cross the river
on horseback. King's Bridge, as you may
know, was fired some months ago by the
rebels, and the flatboat used for ferrying
has been abandoned on account of the ice.
It will afford me pleasure to do what I can
for your comfort and that of your companion. But it is my duty, unfortunately, to

make passing search of your coach; will you pardon me if I do so?"

As he spoke, Captain Yorke advanced to the door and extended his hand to assist the occupant of the vehicle to alight, but Betty, ignoring assistance, attempted to spring past him to the ground. As the willful maiden did so the topknot of her hood caught in a provoking nail of the open door and was violently pulled from her head; and as her lovely, rosy face almost brushed his sleeve, Geoffrey started back with a low cry, —

"*Betty!*"

CHAPTER X

A MAID'S CAPRICE

" Mistress Betty, sir," came the swift whisper in retort, and with so haughty a gesture that Geoffrey stepped back as if he had been struck, while Betty, with a slight inclination of her head, passed on to where Mrs. Seymour stood with Cæsar on the other side of the coach. But if she expected him to follow she was swiftly made aware of her mistake, for Geoffrey merely pursued his intention of searching the pockets of the coach, and when he emerged from it he came, hat in hand, toward the ladies with face more calm and unruffled than Betty's own.

" If you will resume your seats," he said, addressing Mrs. Seymour, without a glance at Betty, who (now that her anger born partly of terror had passed) stole a quick look at him, and as quickly looked away, " I will ride on before you and be waiting at the river; if it be safe, you will cross on

horseback ; if not, on foot, and I shall take
great pleasure in seeing that you reach
King's Bridge Inn in safety." Whereupon
he escorted Mrs. Seymour to the coach, and
when he turned to assist Betty found that
she was in the act of climbing inside by the
other door, where Cæsar stood in attend-
ance.

"What a provoking child it is!" said
Geoffrey to himself as he flung into his saddle, smiling at the recollection of Betty's
rebuke and proud little toss of her head.
"'Mistress Betty'! Very well, so be it ;
and thanks to the star of good fortune which
guided my steps up the road to-day. I
wonder how she comes here, and why," and
Captain Yorke gave his horse the spur as
he galloped on.

Some distance behind him the coach lumbered forward, and Mrs. Seymour's tongue
rattled on gayly. So engrossed was she with
being nearly at her journey's end, and their
good luck at having fallen in with Yorke,
that Betty's silence passed unnoticed.

"To think that we should meet again,"
ran Betty's thoughts. "'Betty,' forsooth!
How dare he use my name so freely! What
would Mrs. Seymour have thought had she

heard him, and how could I possibly have explained with any air of truth unless I told her the whole story — which I would rather die at once than do. He has not changed at all; I should have known him anywhere, even in that hateful scarlet coat, which becomes him so mightily. I wonder if my rebuke was too severe" — and here she became conscious of Mrs. Seymour again.

"Yorke — did not that handsome young officer say his name was Yorke? Why, then he must have some kinship with the Earl of Hardwicke; very probably this young man may be a grandson of the earl. I must ask my sister; she will have some information about it."

"Worse and worse," thought Betty. "A British officer — kinsman of an earl — oh, me, in what a coil am I enveloped! But at least my father knows all, and he would not hold me disloyal."

The coach bumped and jolted along, and finally came to a standstill, while Cæsar's voice was heard addressing some one. Betty looked out of the window and beheld a dismal prospect enough. The bank shelved gradually down to the river, which at this point was narrow, and between them and

the other shore stretched a mixture of snow
and ice; she could distinguish the flat-bot-
tomed boat used for ferrying purposes stuck
fast almost in the middle of the stream.

"How are we to cross?" said Mrs. Seymour dolefully, looking down at her feet.
"I wish I had an extra pair of woolen
stockings to pull over my shoes; the snow
and ice will be cold walking. What are
they doing to the horses?"

"Will it please you to alight, madam?"
said Geoffrey, springing from his saddle at
the door of the coach. "My men are of the
opinion that the ice will not bear so much
weight as your coach with you ladies and
Cæsar in it, but if you can mount your
horses we can lead them and you can cross
in safety. Meanwhile Cæsar can remain
here to guard your property, and when my
men fetch the horses back they can assist
him to transport the coach to the other side.
I hope the plan meets your approbation. It
seems the only feasible one, provided you
ladies can ride without a saddle."

"Bless me," cried Mrs. Seymour, "I shall
surely slip off on the ice! Betty here is a
horsewoman, but, alas! I am not."

"Then we must contrive a way," replied

Geoffrey. "If a blanket be strapped over my saddle I think you can sit on it. — Cæsar, put one of those blankets on my horse instead of yours."

"Oh, that will do nicely; how kind you are, Captain Yorke."

"Will the young lady be able to ride one of your horses?" asked Geoffrey, addressing Mrs. Seymour.

"I can ride anything," said Betty hastily, "for my mare is" — and then she bit her lip and colored brightly as Geoffrey turned toward her.

"You will be quite safe, for I shall lead your horse myself. Let me first attend Mrs. Seymour."

Between terror and small gasps of laughter Mrs. Seymour's mounting was accomplished, and then Geoffrey (artful fellow!) summoned a tall, good-looking trooper from the patrol, and, placing the reins in Mrs. Seymour's hand, gave directions to the man.

"You will hold the horse by the bridle and guide every step with care, letting the lady put her hand on your shoulder to steady herself. Be watchful of the air-holes; I think you know the path well."

"Yes, captain," said the trooper, saluting

respectfully. " Am I to dismount the lady at the Inn?"

"Aye; go down the path before me;" and Geoffrey turned toward Betty, but again the mischievous maid had been too quick for him, and he beheld her already mounted on one of the coach horses, where she sat demurely and at ease awaiting him. Geoffrey seized the bridle and walked slowly down the bank, taking great care of his own steps lest he should by slipping cause the horse to stumble, and in a few seconds they were slowly picking their way over the rough ice. The horse's hoofs crunched into the snow, and Betty held her breath, and a little thrill went over her as she fancied she heard the ice crack under them.

"Oh!" — a half-involuntary cry escaped her, and Geoffrey looked up reassuringly as he stroked the horse's neck and checked him for a brief second. Mrs. Seymour and the trooper were somewhat in advance and had almost reached the opposite shore.

"I — you — that is" — faltered Betty, meekly dropping her eyelids — "Oh, sir, do you really think we shall gain the Inn safely?"

"There is no cause for fear," said Geoffrey coldly. "I know the path;" and he plodded on in silence. Another few rods, a slip, a half halt; but this time it was Yorke who stumbled and fell on one knee.

"Confound my sword," he cried, recovering his feet. "But we are nearly there. See, Mrs. Seymour has gained the road and is riding on to the Inn."

No reply from Betty; in truth, if he had but known it, she dared not trust her voice lest its first sound should be a sob. And Yorke, divided between amusement and wrath at her perversity, vowed he would say no more until she grew less capricious.

The road was well trodden and the snow light as the pair pursued it in silence. The famous hostelry known as King's Bridge Inn was upon the highway going up the Hudson, where Spuyten Duyvil Creek ran down to Harlem River, and many a rendezvous and intrigue had been carried on within its low, wide rooms since the Colonies had declared their independence of British rule. As Yorke approached the door, inside which Mrs. Seymour had already disappeared, a tall, dark man in riding-boots and long coat came hastily forth, and as Betty dropped the reins of her horse he was at her side.

"Oh, Gulian," cried she, stretching out both hands, " don't you know me? 'T is I, Betty Wolcott; have I outgrown your recollection?"

"Betty, indeed," replied Gulian Verplanck, lifting her off the horse, "and right glad am I to welcome you. What good fortune brought you in contact with Captain Yorke's patrol? Had I known of your near approach, I should myself have ridden forth with him, but the air was chilly and I deemed it more prudent to stop at the Inn until to-morrow."

"Since I see you safe" — began Geoffrey, as Betty half turned toward him.

"You do not know whom you have so kindly assisted," broke in Verplanck; "this is Mistress Betty Wolcott, sister to my wife. Betty, I present to you Captain Geoffrey Yorke, aide to Sir Henry Clinton, and my friend."

Betty executed her most stately and deepest courtesy, and Yorke swept his hat gracefully to the very ground; but as she raised her eyes she said, with a mischievous glance, " I am pleased to learn the name of this gentleman. Sir, I thank you," and giving him a little gracious nod, Betty vanished inside the open door of the Inn.

"Verplanck," called Geoffrey, as his friend was about to follow her, "I shall go directly back to the city, for Sir Henry has to make ready dispatches for England and will need me. Mrs. Seymour's coach will be brought over at once : my men are assisting the negro servant in the transit. Do you follow me shortly ?"

"Unless the ladies are too weary we will go at once, for I can obtain fresh horses here and the Inn seems somewhat overcrowded to stop the night. But if you are in haste, Yorke, do not wait."

"Very well, then, I will depart at once. But you must have at least two of my men as escort for the coach and yourself. You know there are plenty of footpads outlying the city."

"I accept the escort gladly," said Verplanck. "Farewell, then, and my hearty thanks."

Betty and Mrs. Seymour had been ushered into a small bedchamber, where they were making some slight changes of dress when Gulian Verplanck knocked at the door and informed them that the coach would shortly be ready for the continuation of their journey. Betty followed him back into the waiting-room, where a good fire was burning, and Verplanck sought to find a seat for her near the hearth. The room was occupied by perhaps a dozen persons, all men : some troopers, and a group of traders whose bundles of furs, lying on the floor beside the table where they were partaking of glasses of home-brewed beer, told their occupation. On one settle, close by the chimney, sat an old man, somewhat ragged, who had fallen asleep with his head resting against his bundle and stick, which shared the bench with him ; on the other sat a slight youth dressed in homespun clothing, who instantly rose as Betty approached, and offered her his seat.

"I am warmed enough," he said, as Verplanck gave brief thanks ; "besides there is room here. Wake up, grandfather," and he gave the sleeping man a gentle push as he squeezed himself down beside him.

"Stay here till the coach is ready, Betty," said Verplanck. "Mrs. Seymour will join you presently," and he departed to hasten the hostlers, who could be heard outside, evidently engaged in harnessing the horses they were to use.

Betty looked around her curiously. The

room, with its low ceilings, dark rafters,
and sanded floor, was fairly tidy, and, in the
light and shade of the shifting fire, picturesque and strange. A short, thick-set man,
evidently the host, a comfortable-looking
Dutchman, bustled in and out, giving directions in a perfectly audible aside to a maid,
who wore a queer straight cap and brought
in trays of beer to the thirsty party of
traders. A little boy in one corner was
playing with some nails and a pewter plate ;
each time he dropped the nails, making a
jingling noise, the landlord said, " Hush,
there, Hans," in a loud whisper, to which the
child paid no attention. Betty wondered
if it was his son, and felt as if she would
like to go over and play with him ; and
then thought, with a half-homesick longing,
of Moppet and the dear New England
home. Far, far away ran Betty's thoughts,
as minute after minute sped along and no
one came to disturb her reverie. So engrossed was she that not even a low, but
distinctly spoken " *hist*," which came from
the settle near her, aroused her until it
had been given the third time. Then she
started ; there was something familiar in
the sound — was any one speaking to her ?

" Hist ! do not look this way," whispered
a voice which came from the pair opposite
her on the other side of the chimney.
" Contrive to pass near me as you go out
— be cautious ! "

" All ready, Betty ?" said Mrs. Seymour's gay voice, as she came across the
room toward her. " Where is Mr. Verplanck ? "

" Here," answered Gulian, from the other
door. " Hasten, Betty ; the horses are eager
to be off."

" I am coming," replied Betty, as she rose
hurriedly and dropped her silk reticule
directly in front of the mysterious pair on
the settle. The boy darted up, giving the
bag a furtive kick which sent it under
the bench.

" I 'll reach it for you, madam," he said
aloud, diving down for it as Betty paused a
brief second. The old man stirred sleepily,
raised his head from his bundle, and keen
bright eyes that Betty knew well flashed
into hers as he whispered rapidly : —

" Show no alarm, Betty, but no matter
how or where you see me, make no sign of
recognition."

" Here 's your bag," said the boy, springing to his feet. But Betty, never stopping to thank him, ran rapidly across the room, out of the door, and darted into the waiting coach, afraid to even glance behind her, her heart sinking with dismay, for the voice and eyes of that ragged old man were those of her brother Oliver!

CHAPTER XI

ON THE COLLECT

" Peter, Peter," said Grandma Effingham in a tone of gentle remonstrance, " if thee would only let the ball alone Tabitha would keep quiet."

" Stop it, Peter," said Betty, from the doorway, as the irrepressible youngster rolled over and over on the rug, himself, the gray cat, and the ball of gray yarn hopelessly entangled. " Much you deserve all the stockings that grandma knits for you so perseveringly ; just look at the condition of that ball " — and by a skillful flank movement she rescued the yarn as Tabitha's pranks and Peter's tumble came to a hasty conclusion, and the chief culprit gained his feet and began to apologize for his frolic, as the cat fled through the door.

" I was just waiting for you, Betty ; you girls take such a long time to put on your capes and furbelows. I 'll warrant Kitty will detain us when we stop for her, and we

must hasten, for the sun will not stay up
much longer. Just let me find my muffler
and my skates," and off tore Peter, while
Betty tucked up her gown preparatory to an
afternoon on the Collect Pond, whose frozen
surface was the resort of all fashionable
New York, both those who joined the skaters, and others who watched them from the
surrounding banks, making a gay, bright
winter scene for the spectators as well as the
participants.

It was some three weeks since Betty's
eventful journey, and as the strangeness of
her new home and surroundings wore off
she was beginning to enjoy herself. First
of all, the dear happiness of being once
more with Clarissa, who had brightened and
strengthened each day since her arrival;
then Grandma Effingham's storehouse of
anecdotes and pleasant stories, to which
Betty listened with delight and the respectful deference that youth of those days paid
to age; and last (though Betty would have
denied it stoutly) the frequent visits to the
Verplancks of a certain tall soldier, whose
red coat made her eyes sparkle with disdain, even while her heart beat quicker at
sound of his voice. Truly, Betty's soul

was torn within her, and for every smile that
Yorke succeeded in winning he was sure
to receive such dainty snubs, such mischievous flouting following swiftly after, that he
almost despaired of ever carrying the out-
works, much less the citadel of the willful
maid's heart.

Kitty Cruger had received Betty most
cordially, but the acquaintance had not yet
progressed toward intimacy. On several
occasions when Betty had been especially
teasing, Yorke had seen fit to retaliate by
seeking Kitty's side, and, although he was
far from suspecting it, he had thus piqued
his little lady-love extremely. For Kitty
was a reigning belle, and the toast of the
British officers as she had been of the Continentals, and she liked Yorke and Yorke's
attentions. If Betty had only known whose
face came oftenest in Kitty's dreams, and
that a blue sword-knot was her most cherished possession, perhaps the dawning jeal-
ousy which she felt toward her would never
have existed. Who can say?

The winter had set in with great rigor,
and the troops had even crossed on the ice
from Staten Island to the city; sad tales
reached Betty's watchful ears of privations

endured in the army of General Washington, and it made her cheeks burn and tingle to hear the jests and laughter of the Tory guests who visited the house, at the expense of the so-called " rebels " against King George.   Of Oliver, Betty had no sign; whether he had been in the city and accomplished whatever mission he had in view, she knew not.   She did not dare to confide in Clarissa, for even had her sister's health permitted, Betty deemed it scarcely safe to put her to the test of loyalty as between husband and brother.

All these thoughts and many more were crowding Betty's brain as she ran down the steps of the Verplanck mansion and followed Peter toward Queen Street, where Kitty lived.   The sun shone brightly and the air was crisp and clear: Betty looked charming in her dainty hood, tied with a rose-colored ribbon which nestled softly under her chin and played at confining the dancing curls.   Contrary to Peter's expectations, Kitty was watching for them, and they proceeded with some speed along the snowy streets until they reached the Minetta Water, as the small stream was called which wound its way across the Lispenard Meadows, and connected the " Collect " (or Fresh Water Pond) with the Hudson River. At the end of Great Queen Street was a wooden bridge, and crossing it, the little party continued up Magazine Street until they reached the Collect Pond, on two sides of which were low buildings of various kinds, being ropewalks, furnaces, tanneries, and breweries, all run by water from the pond. Betty thought she should some day like to come out and investigate them with Peter ; they were not very sightly, but they might prove interesting. These buildings shut out the view, and until Betty stood on the very bank she had no idea how brilliant a scene the Collect presented. The ground on the north side between them and Broadway rose to the height of a hundred feet, and this hillside was covered with spectators who were watching the skaters with which the ice was alive. Among the crowd were many women of fashion, muffled in their furs, carrying huge muffs to keep their fingers warm, and scarlet uniforms, dotted here and there, served to heighten the effect of brilliancy and animation. As they turned the corner of a furnace whose big chimney had sheltered them for a moment, a young man darted up the bank and greeted Kitty.

"How late you are," he said reproachfully. " Philip Livingston and I have been watching for you this hour. The ice is in fine condition ; may I put on your skates?"

While young De Lancey was thus engaged Peter and Betty were making ready also. Up in the Litchfield hills, where the winter set in early and lasted late, Betty had learned to use her skates well, and she and her brother Oliver had been the best skaters in the township when she was hardly more than a child. Even the timid Pamela had gained boldness and dexterity on the clear, frozen pond ; and therefore when Betty, with the ease of a practiced skater, glided off without assistance, Peter flew after her in round-eyed amazement.

" I say, Betty," he exclaimed, breathless with his effort to catch her, " how you do fly ! My eye ! there is n't one of these New York dames or maids who can equal you," and he chuckled with triumph as Betty began to execute some very difficult motions which she and Oliver had often practiced together.

" Give me your hand, Peter : there, now, glide this way, and take the outside roll — oh ! have a care ; if you turn like that you will surely catch your skate in mine. That 's better; now cross hands, and go gently; see, I am cutting a face on the ice."

Surely enough, as Peter glanced behind he saw a gigantic profile grow on the smooth surface beneath Betty's little foot, and the skaters around them paused to wonder and admire.

"There," said Betty, making a final flourish, "come back to the bank and let us find Kitty." But as they flew along Betty saw a familiar red coat appear beside Kitty's advancing figure, so dropping Peter's hand she dashed off in an opposite direction. She headed for the north bank, which was less crowded, but slacked her speed a little, fearing an air-hole, as she debated which way to turn.

"Mistress Betty," said a voice just behind her, and with a little start she realized that the obnoxious scarlet coat had reached her side, "will you skate a turn with me down the pond?"

"Surely," and Betty's most roguish smile beamed into Yorke's eyes as she wheeled toward him. "Perhaps you will try a race with me, Captain Yorke?"

"With pleasure, and for what stakes?" returned Yorke, bending down to secure a strap which he felt loosen.

"I meant but a trial of speed to the bridge there, where we cross the Minetta Water. A stake? Well, name it."

"A knot of rose-colored ribbon," said Yorke softly.

"Another!" cried Betty unguardedly, and could have promptly bitten her tongue for the betrayal of her thought.

"Ah, then you do remember?" asked Yorke. "In what have I so deeply offended that I can scarce gain speech of you? Why do you flout one who longs to show you his devotion?"

"You forget, sir," said Betty coldly, "the coat you wear. Do you fancy that scarlet commends itself to a rebel maid like me, or that the cause you represent can be aught but hateful to a loyal Wolcott?"

"Betty, Betty! I do beseech you" —

"Nay, we will put entreaty outside the question. A race, I think I said, Captain Yorke. I will make the stake that self-same bow of rose-color — if you have kept it so long."

An indignant flush dyed Yorke's face. "So be it," he said briefly, and in a flash they were off; she, graceful, and almost like a winged bird, as she sped along; and he, tall, straight, and muscular, with a long, staying stroke, which impelled Betty's admiration. The distance to the bridge was a good half mile, and the spectators on the hill presently perceived the racing pair, and from the cries and shouts which arose she learned, to her added chagrin, that they were seen, and their trial of speed would be eagerly followed. On flew Betty, so intent upon reaching her goal that she never noticed how Yorke crept closer and closer; they were almost to the bridge, when his voice sounded at her shoulder : —

" You should have the race, sweetheart, but I cannot part with the ribbon," and with a sudden rush Yorke darted past her and gained the bridge barely three seconds in advance.

" Forgive me," he had time to whisper, as Betty stood still, with flashing eyes and half-quivering lip, while they waited for Peter, Kitty, and Philip Livingston, who had followed them down the course; " 't was too dear a stake for me to lose." But as the words left his lips, to his astonishment and delight, with all a child's frankness, Betty gave him her hand.

" Nay, you won the race fairly, and Betty Wolcott craves your pardon."

"Oh, my eye!" shouted Peter, as he flung himself between them; "'t was the prettiest race of the season, was it not, Kitty? Do, do try a game with the rest of us, and I 'll be your hurlie myself."

A hurlie, be it known, was a small boy or man who, in the fashion of a ball-game of the day, propelled the balls along the icy surface of the pond with a long, sharp-pointed stick, and the race was accorded to whoever first caught the ball, — often a trial of both speed and endurance when the course was a long one.

"Are you deserting me, Peter?" put in Kitty playfully; "the other hurlies are busy with the De Lancey party; we must have two or three at least."

Yorke moved a step forward; his first impulse was to offer his services to Kitty, as he had done before, but some fine instinct warned him not to jeopardize his half-recon-ciliation with Betty, and before he could speak, Philip Livingston whistled to a tall, slight lad who was standing looking at them from the bank close at hand. In response the lad ran down, leaped on the ice, and said pleasantly, —

"Your pleasure, sir. Did you call me?"

"Can you drive a ball for me?" asked Philip; "if so, I'll promise you a shilling for an hour of your time."

"Indeed I will," said the boy; "but let me first go tell Jim Bates, there, who maybe will be returning to Paulus Hook, and I'll just bid him wait for me over yonder in the tan-yard until you gentlefolks have had your game."

Off darted the new recruit, and was seen to join a man wearing the wide hat and somewhat greasy garb of a fisherman, who, after a few words, nodded assent, and with somewhat slouching gait proceeded leisurely across the bridge in the direction of the tan-yard referred to. Amid much laughter the game began; some other acquaintances came down the bank and joined them, and presently Betty found herself darting over the ice hither and thither, following Peter's purposely erratic course, and pursuing the ball, determined this time to outdo Yorke, who followed her every motion, and whom she again began to tease and laugh at. But to Yorke anything was better than her scorn or displeasure, and when, by a lucky stroke and a quick turn of her skates, Betty bent down and captured the elusive ball, he was the first to raise a shout of triumph, in which the merry party joined with the heartiness of good-fellowship and breeding.

It was growing dark and cold as Betty climbed up the bank and seated herself on a pile of boards, while Peter unstrapped her skates. As she looked up, she saw Yorke and Philip Livingston talking with the boy who had been hurlie for Kitty, and it crossed her mind to wonder where Kitty had vanished. So she rose to her feet and walked leisurely along with Peter toward the tanyard and turned the corner of the furnace chimney. As she did so, she almost stumbled against a man, who drew back suddenly: on the other side stood Kitty, and Betty distinctly saw a piece of white paper pass from Kitty's muff into the hand of the stranger, whom she instantly recognized as the greasy fisherman who had crossed the bridge half an hour before.

CHAPTER XII

A FACE ON THE WALL

BETTY sat in her favorite seat, a low, three-legged cricket, on the side farthest from the fire in Clarissa's little morning-room; it was the day before Christmas, and Betty's fingers were busy tying evergreens into small bunches and wreaths. Of these a large hamperful stood at her elbow, and Peter was cutting away the smaller branches, with a face of importance.

"So you have never kept Christmas before," said he, pausing in his cheerful whistle, which he kept up under his breath like a violin obligato to his whittling of boughs; "and you don't believe in Kris Kringle and his prancing reindeers? My, what fun we boys had up in the old Beverwyck at Albany last year," and Peter chuckled at the recollection of past pranks. "Down here in the city it is chiefly New Year day which is observed, but thank fortune Gulian is sufficiently Dutch to believe in St. Nicholas."

"Yes?" murmured Betty, her thoughts far
away as she wondered what Moppet was
doing up in the Litchfield hills, and whether
Oliver had got back safely to the army
again. Surely, he had cautioned her not to
recognize him, but luckily her fortitude had
not been put to proof. And then she wondered what secret mission Kitty had been
engaged upon that day at Collect Pond.
Somehow Kitty and she had been more confidential since then; and one night, sitting
by the fire in Betty's room, Kitty had confessed that she too was a rebel — yes, a
sturdy, unswerving rebel, true to the Colonies and General Washington, and Betty's
warm heart had gone forth toward her from
that very moment.

"Clarissa has a huge crock full of *olykeoks*
in the pantry," pursued Peter, to whom the
Dutch dainty was sufficiently toothsome;
"and Pompey has orders to brew a fine
punch made of cider and lemons for the servants, and oh! Betty, do you know that
Miranda has a new follower? His name
is Sambo, and he comes from Breucklen
Heights; he has been practicing a dance
with her, and old Jan Steen, the Dutch fiddler, has promised to come and play for

them and their friends in the kitchen, and
for my part I think there will be more fun
there than at Clarissa's card-party — don't
you? Wake up, Betty; I don't believe
you 've heard one word I 've been saying."

" Indeed I have," replied Betty, returning
to her present surroundings with a start.
" A dance, Peter? Why, it seems to me
the servants have great liberty here."

" Don't you give yours a holiday up in
New England? I thought you had negro
servants as well as we?"

" So we do; you know that Miranda is
the daughter of our old cook, Chloe. She
came here with Clarissa when she was a
bride; oh, we have a few negro servants in
dear New England, Peter, but not so many
as here. Gulian told me that there are some
three thousand slaves owned in the city and
its environs. But our negroes go to church
and pray; they do not dance, and I know
Chloe would be shocked with Miranda's flippant ways. She was ever opposed to dancing."

" Don't be prim, Betty."

" I — prim?" — and Betty went off into
a shout of girlish laughter, as she flung a
pine needle at Peter, who dodged it success-

fully; " that I live to hear myself called
what I have so often dubbed Pamela. Fie,
Peter, let Miranda dance if she will: I
should love to see her. It would be far
more amusing than cards."

"Betty," said Peter, edging nearer her
and lowering his voice to a whisper, " I
heard that the Sons of Liberty had another
placard up near the Vly Market last night,
and that Sir Henry Clinton is in great
wrath because they are growing daring
again. My! would n't I just like to see one
of them; but they say (so Pompey told me)
that they are all around us in different dis-
guises. That 's why they 're so difficult to
catch: it would go hard with them if the
Hessians lay hands on the author of the placards."

" But they will not; I heard Gulian say
only last night that the cleverness with
which the placards are prepared and placed
was wonderful. Who tells you these things,
Peter? Do have a care, for we are under
Gulian's roof, and he would be very angry
if he knew that your and my sympathies are
all on the side of the Whigs."

"Oh, I hear things," murmured Peter
evasively. Then whispering in Betty's ear,

"Did you ever hear Kitty speak of Billy the fiddler?"

"There's no one within hearing," said Betty, as she finished her twelfth wreath and laid it carefully on the floor beside her cricket. "Get the other big branch outside the door, and sit down here close by me while you pull the twigs off; then you can tell me safely, for Clarissa is sleeping, and she will call me when she wakes. Of course I never heard of the man you mention."

Peter threw back his head in a prolonged chuckle, as he followed Betty's instructions and edged his cricket close to her elbow.

"Man! — well, he's more like a monkey than anything. He only comes to my shoulder, and yet he's old enough to be my father."

"A dwarf, do you mean?"

"No, not precisely; the boys call him a manikin, for he's not deformed; only very, very small; not above four feet high. He is Dutch and has been a drummer, it's whispered, in General Washington's army. They say he was in the battle of Harlem Lane, and beat the rally for our troops when Knowlton fell. The Vly boys are great friends with him."

"But I thought you were at daggers
drawn with the boys of the Vly Market,
Peter? Surely, you told me blood-curdling
tales of the fights between them and you
Broadway boys?"

"Oh, aye, but that's for right of way,
and don't mean much except when we are
actually punching each other's heads. Billy
can tell great yarns; how his eyes flash
when he speaks of the prison ships, though
I only heard him once, when Jan Steen was
talking foolish Tory stuff."

"Do you think 'Billy the fiddler,' as you
call him, is one of the Sons of Liberty?"

"H-u-s-h!" and Peter looked fearfully
around. "I don't dare say, but I'm sure
he's true and steady. Betty, I wish I was
a little taller; if I were I'd run away some
fine morning and go for a drummer boy
with General Washington."

Betty looked up with affectionate eyes at
the sturdy urchin. "I know how you feel,
Peter; but wait a bit. It's sad and dis-
heartening enough now, God knows, but
perhaps better days may dawn for the patriots. My father says we must keep up our
hearts as best we can, and trust in God and
the Continental Congress. Did I tell you

how we moulded the bullets last summer? We kept the tally, and over forty-two thousand cartridges were made from the statue of King George, so the women of Litchfield have contributed their aid to the cause in good practical fashion."

"Aye, that was fine! It must have been jolly fun, too."

"It was very hot," said Betty, laughing; "we tried it in our big kitchen, but finally had to melt the lead in larger kettles hung over a crane in the shed down in the orchard. Aunt Euphemia thought we would fire the house, and for many nights Miss Bidwell and she, protected by Reuben with a lantern, paraded the place before closing up, hunting for stray sparks which she fancied might fly in the wrong direction."

"What a lot this hamper holds," said Peter, diving down into it. "You've made enough wreaths to decorate the rooms, I'm sure, and your hands are getting black."

"Never mind my hands; soap and water will cleanse them. Clarissa wants a 'real English Christmas,' she said, and poor dear! she shall have it. It does my heart good to see her brighten and glow like her old pretty self."

"You can thank Captain Yorke for putting the 'real English Christmas' into her head; there's a fine Tory for you, Betty. Sometimes I forget he's one of our foes — he's almost nice enough to be a patriot."

"He thinks he is one, Peter; he owes his loyalty to his king, and were less than a man not to give his services where ordered."

"Ha, ha!" quoth Peter teasingly; "you'll be as bad as Kitty presently."

"How so?" returned Betty, biting her lip as she turned her face away from Peter's roguish eyes.

"Why, Kitty had a walk-over course with the scarlet coats until you came, and Captain Yorke was one of her gallants. But now I find him at your elbow whenever you give him half a chance. But I've seen you snub him well, too; you girls are such changeable creatures. I'd not have a scarlet coat dancing around after me if I were you, Betty:" and Peter endeavored to look sage and wise as he cocked his head on one side like a conceited sparrow. What reply Betty might have made to his pertness was uncertain, but at that moment both doors of the room opened and Clarissa entered by one as Kitty flew in the other.

"How industrious you are," cried Kitty, as she bade them all good-day; "the rooms will be a bower of green, such as Captain Yorke tells about. I came, Clarissa, to beg a note of invitation for Peggy Van Dam. She has but just returned from Albany, and will be mightily pleased to be bidden to your card-party."

"I wondered if she would be in time," said Clarissa, seating herself at her claw-legged, brass-mounted writing-table. "Has she changed much, Kitty — not that I mean" — and Clarissa's sentence ended in a laugh.

"There was room for it," finished Kitty. "No, she is just the same: aping youth, with the desire to conceal age."

"Oh, Kitty, that's the severest speech I ever knew you guilty of!"

"Ill-natured, aye," quoth Kitty, with a comical sigh; "the world's awry this morning and I must vent my crossness on somebody, so let it be Peggy. But if I can carry her your note it will atone for my peevish speech a dozen times, for is not Captain Sir John Faulkner coming, and you know as well as all of us that Peggy's airs and graces are most apparent in his company."

Betty looked quickly up into Kitty's face
as she rattled on gayly, and detected an
air of trouble and anxiety that was most
unusual. And as they presently followed
Clarissa downstairs, she paused at the landing and slid her little fingers into Kitty's as
she whispered : —

" What's amiss ? You are worried, I
perceive ; can I help you ? " Kitty started,
and turning her head over her shoulder said
softly : —

" Not now, but I know that you are true-
hearted and quick-witted ; I dare not say one
word more," and with an affectionate pressure, she dropped Betty's hand and ran
swiftly down the staircase.

The drawing-room in the Verplanck mansion was high of ceiling, a spacious, stately
room, and its quaint, straight-backed chairs,
stuffed ottomans, and carved mahogany sofas
were the acme of elegance of those days.
The highly polished floor had received extra
attention from Pompey and his assistants,
while the mirrors shone brightly and reflected the candles of the brass sconces
on either side of their glittering surfaces.
Betty, at Clarissa's request, superintended
the placing of the card - tables, and also

that of a huge silver salver, on which the tiny cups for chocolate and the tall glasses for mulled wine would be served from a table in the dining-room early in the evening before supper; also a famous bowl of Indian china, where hot caudle would appear, caudle being an English compound with which Betty was not familiar. Peter explained it to her with due regard to detail; and smacked his lips over the kettle as it smoked away on Dinah's kitchen table, where he had invited Betty to come out and see it.

"Dinah makes a sort of posset first, of oaten-meal, and then she puts in coriander seeds, and raisins, all carefully stoned (I ought to know that, for I helped her one mortal hour last night and got my fingers sticky with the plagued stones), and some cloves in a muslin bag, which are let lie till the caudle boils, and then removed, and last of all, just as it's ready to serve, she pops in a good half bottle of cognac — my! but it's prime!" and Peter cut a pigeon-wing and gave a regular Mohawk war-whoop, as he danced around the kitchen and disappeared through the door just in time to avoid Dinah's wet dishcloth, which she sent spinning at his close-cropped pate.

Betty stood in her small chamber at six o'clock that evening, contemplating her gown with critical eye. Parties in those days were early affairs, and in New York were known to assemble as early as half past seven. The lanterns which hung outside every seventh house for the purpose of lighting the streets were lit by the watchmen at half past six, for the winter days were short, and the denizens of Wall Street were wont to pick their way most carefully since the great fire, the débris of which in many instances was still left to disfigure the sites where had stood stately mansions. Betty deliberated for some minutes; here were two gowns: one must be worn to-night for her dear Clarissa; the other kept for the De Lancey ball, an event over which all fashionable New York was agog, and which would take place on New Year's night, just one week ahead.

On the high, four-posted bed lay the gowns; one, which had been her mother's, was a white satin petticoat, over which was worn a slip of India muslin covered with fine embroidery, so daintily worked that it was almost like lace itself. The dames of Connecticut, and, indeed, of all New Eng-

land, were much more sober in their dress
than those of New York, where the Dutch
love of color still lingered, and the Tories
clung to the powdered heads and gay fash-
ions of the English court circles. The other
gown (which in her secret soul Betty longed
to wear) had been given her by Gulian, who
was the most generous of men, and who admired his pretty sister-in-law far more than
he would have told her. A ship had recently
arrived from England bringing him a box
of gowns and gewgaws ordered long since
for his wife, and of these Gulian had made
Clarissa happy by bidding her bestow on
Betty a gown such as he considered fitting
for a grand festivity like the De Lanceys'
New Year ball.

" Alack ! " sighed the pretty maid to herself, as she contemplated the white satin,
" I will not even raise the paper which
contains Clarissa's present, for both she and
Gulian have set their hearts upon my wearing it on New Year's day, so 't is useless to
fill my breast with discontent when I have
so good a gown as this to wear to-night.
The skirt is a little frayed — oh ! how vexing ! " and Betty flew to her reticule for
needle and thread to set a timely stitch ;

" now that will not show when the muslin
slip goes over." Another anxious moment,
and with a sigh of relief Betty slipped on
the short waist with its puffed sleeves and
essayed to pin the fichu daintily around her
neck. Then she dived down to the very
depths of a chest of drawers, whence she
produced a small box, and out of this came
a single string of pearls, — the pearls which
her mother had worn upon her wedding-
day, and Pamela had pressed into her hand
at parting. Next, Betty with cautious steps,
candle in hand, approached the mirror,
which graced the farther end of her tiny
chamber, and holding it at arm's length
surveyed herself as far as she could see,
which was not below her dainty waist, as
suited the dimensions of the mirror afore-
said.

"I am too white," thought Betty, with a
little frown, all unconscious of her lovely
coloring and exquisite red-gold hair, which,
guiltless of powder, was massed as usual on
top of her head and clustered in wayward
little curls on the nape of her snowy neck
and over her white forehead; "but never
mind," — with childlike philosophy, — "my
gown for the New Year ball has both breast

and shoulder knots of rose-color; I wish I dare steal one for to-night! But perhaps Clarissa would not be pleased, so I will descend as I am. I hear Peter clattering on the staircase; he is no doubt superintending the servants' dance," and Betty extinguished her candle and tripped lightly down past Clarissa's door.

From the sounds and lights she became aware that she was late, and had lingered too long over her toilet, so she hesitated for a brief moment as she reached the door of the drawing-room, where she could see Clarissa and Grandma Effingham standing with a number of guests, both dames and gentlemen. As she paused on the threshold a graceful, girlish picture, a tall form emerged from the dim shades of the hall, and a hand met hers.

"Mistress Betty, I salute you," said Geoffrey Yorke, bowing low, "and may I also beg your acceptance of a bunch of clove pinks? They were grown by my Dutch landlady in a box kept carefully in her kitchen window, and I know not whether she or I have watched them the more carefully, as I wished to be so fortunate as to have them bloom for you to-night."

" For me ? " said Betty, in a delighted
whisper, turning such glowing eyes upon
him that the young man fell more madly in
love with her than ever. " How kind ! —
and at this season ? Oh, they are sweet,
and recall the garden walk at home. Indeed, sir, I thank you," and scarcely thinking what she did, in her pleasure at his
pretty attention, she thrust the bunch of
pinks in her fichu, where they lay close
to her white throat and gave her toilet the
one touch of color for which she had longed.
Small wonder that Geoffrey's handsome face
lit up with triumph, or that Clarissa said to
herself as the pair approached her, Betty
dimpling with smiles, " What a charming
couple they make ! I wonder if my father
would object ? "

This was Clarissa's first appearance in
society for many months, and the warmth
with which she was greeted showed how
large a place the New England girl had
made in the regard of her husband's friends.
The party was given chiefly for Betty, that
she might have plenty of partners at the
New Year ball ; and although these were
mostly young people, there was also a
goodly sprinkling of dames and dowagers,

who smiled approvingly when Betty was
presented to them, before seating themselves at the all-absorbing card - tables.
Cards were much the mode of the day, and
an hour or more was given to them ; then
as the metheglin (a delicious beverage made
of honey) and the mulled wine was passed,
the younger portion of the company began
moving through the suite of three rooms,
breaking up into small groups as they did
so.

Peter, who had constituted himself master
of ceremonies for the fun in low life which
was going on in the kitchen, darted up to
Betty as she stood talking with Philip Livingston.

" They 're just going to begin to dance,"
he said. " Miranda is perked out in a
wonderful pink gown, and Aunt Dinah has
her best turban on her head. Do, Betty,
persuade some of the company to come out
and see the negroes dance. Don't you hear
the music beginning ? "

Surely enough the distant scraping of the
violin could be heard, and Betty, seizing
Kitty by the hand, tripped up to Clarissa
and repeated Peter's request. Clarissa hesitated an instant.

" Oh, Gulian," cried Betty, catching hold
of her brother-in-law as he came forward,
" may we not visit the kitchen and see the
servants dance? Captain Yorke tells me
that is what is done in England on Christmas Eve, and I am sure it would afford us
all a new amusement."

Artful Betty! She knew full well that
any suggestion of England and English
ways would appeal to Gulian, and Yorke,
who followed closely at her side, threw the
potent weight of his opinion in the scale by
saying quietly : —

" I am told your slaves have the very
poetry of motion, Verplanck; permit me
to escort Mistress Betty to the servants'
hall."

" Servants' hall! " whispered Betty mischievously to Yorke, as Gulian led the way
with Clarissa ; " we have nothing so fine in
our humble colonies, sir ; our kitchens must
serve for our dusky retainers."

" You know I did not mean " — he began
reproachfully. But seeing Betty's laughing
eyes, he added, with a smile : —

" Nay, you shall not tease me into vexing
you to-night if I can avoid it ; I will strive
to train my tongue to please you."

The kitchen presented a quaint and most picturesque appearance. It was a low, wide room, and around the wall ran shelves and dressers, on which the pewter plates and copper covers shone with such fine polish that one could almost see in their surfaces as in a mirror. Between these hung bunches of herbs and strings of bright-hued peppers, and in and out on the walls, and above, from the rafters, were Christmas greens, all arranged by the servants themselves, with that unerring eye for grace and color which is an attribute of the colored race. Aunt Dinah, the presiding genius of the kitchen, stood at one end of the room. Her large and portly person was clothed in a gay cotton print of many colors : and upon her head was twisted a bright silk handkerchief, with a most rakish-looking bow which reposed over her left ear. The Verplanck slaves, some twelve of them, were augmented in numbers by those of the Ludlow, De Lancey, and De Peyster families, and half filled the spacious kitchen as they stood back in rows, courtesying and bowing, showing their white teeth in smiles and low laughter, as they recognized some " young massa," or " ole madam " among the gentle-

men and dames who smiled back upon their
faithful, kindly faces.

The dance began with a special contra-
dance, in which the performers copied with
great exactness the profound bows and deep
courtesies of the period, mimicking their
masters and mistresses with curious gro-
tesque grace. At the extreme end of the
room, near Aunt Dinah, sat the fiddler,
wielding his bow with an extra flourish befitting the occasion. Jan Steen was a well-
known character, and his coming was looked
upon as a special favor, only accorded to
the servants because they belonged to the
Verplancks, a family greatly honored and
beloved among the Dutch settlers of Man-
hattan Island.

After the contra-dance was concluded,
amid the applause and laughter of the spectators, four young slaves were singled out
from the others, and took their places on
the floor. Two of these were girls, pretty
mulattoes, and two young, bright-colored
negro men as their partners. To rather slow
music they went through with a rhythmic
dance, in which their figures swayed to and
fro, chiefly from the waist, a gliding serpen-
tine dance, evidently copied from the slaves

of Martinique, and brought to New York by the French families. And then, to Peter's great delight, came the event of the evening, in his eyes, — the dance of Miranda with her new admirer from Breucklen Heights.

" Miranda is my maid," explained Clarissa to Madam De Lancey and Mrs. Morris, as they waited for the performers to take their places. " I fetched her from Connecticut when I was married, and she is, as you see, very pretty and most graceful. The dance is a species of Spanish dance, I fancy, for it is done with two scarfs of red and yellow ; I purchased the stuff a year ago from a Dutch peddler, and Miranda begged it of me last week."

" Cousin Clarissa," said Peter, rushing up, " we will want more light to enable you to see this ; the candles are getting low. With your permission, may Pompey light the big lantern on the wall ? "

About the middle of the kitchen hung a lantern which had once been used for illuminating purposes outside the mansion. It contained a piece of tin which acted as a reflector ; and Peter, who had never yet had the pleasure of seeing it lit, had amused himself that very morning by putting in the candles for which it was prepared, and informed Aunt Dinah that he meant to light it by way of a climax to the festivities of Christmas Eve.

"The big lantern?" replied Clarissa; "it has not been lit this three years."

"I made it ready this morning; oh, do say yes."

"Certainly," said Clarissa, smiling; "but tell Pompey to be careful, Peter."

Off flew Peter, and up on a bench mounted Pompey, nothing loth to add dignity to the scene by illuminating it. Jan Steen drew his bow across his violin with a long, sweet note, and out on the floor glided Miranda, holding the hand of a tall, athletic-looking young negro, whose motions were grace itself. They began at the top of the room, holding the scarfs aloft, and slowly made their way down until they were in the centre, when the full light gleamed strongly upon their raised arms, their heads well up. Soft murmurs of applause began to steal around the room. Betty stood with Captain Yorke and Kitty directly under the lantern, beating time with her fan.

"How graceful they are," said Yorke softly. "See, even their shadows on the wall opposite are picturesque and wild. How distinct the faces are!"

"Silhouettes!" burst in Kitty; "have you seen the pictures made by the new artist who came from Albany? Some folks like to be done thus, but for me I do not care for a black profile of my own face. They are cut skillfully enough in paper, however."

Betty, wondering what had possessed Kitty to set off on an animated description of silhouettes, looked up at the wall, and then her heart almost stood still. That fine, high forehead, the curving lips, the nose, with its clear-cut nostrils, — not even the disfiguring woolly wig, stiff collar, and blackened face and hands could disguise them to her. She gazed with sickening apprehension at the dancers; how often she had seen Oliver dancing with Miranda when they were children together at home, the performance usually taking place in the garret, for fear of scoldings upon the sinfulness of dancing from Chloe, Miranda's mother; oh, how did he dare do this here, where any moment might bring discovery and death? Why, why, had she failed to see and recognize him! his disguise was very perfect, and yet —

The applause rang out heartily as the

dancers tripped faster and faster; Betty
wondered if her torture would ever end.
Perhaps it had only begun, for Oliver had
said —

"Mistress Betty," spoke Yorke, and his
voice was low and very tender, " may I offer
you my arm? A glass of mulled wine would,
I think, be of service to you." Stumbling a
little in her agitation, Betty slipped through
the door with him, on into the dining-room,
where he placed her in a corner of the wide
sofa and fetched the wine.

"Drink it, every drop," he said, smiling
down at her with a masterful look in his
dark eyes that Betty had never seen before.
"Sweetheart, trust me, and sit here till I
return."

Betty sipped her wine and the truant
color came back to her cheeks, as she saw
him vanish through the door.

"Have I grown a coward?" she thought
indignantly. " I was brave up in the Litchfield hills — how dare I fail now! Captain
Yorke must have seen — and yet, how could
he know Oliver's face sufficiently well?
Ah," — and Betty almost cried out, — " it
is I, miserable I, who have betrayed my
brother. We are so strongly alike that " —

" Mistress Betty," — Yorke was at her side again, — " I left you to bestow a few shillings on yonder fellow who danced so well, but I could not find him, and Mistress Kitty Cruger tells me he left at once for Breuck- len Heights, whence he came, as there is a party crossing before daybreak. I trust you are better; the air was close in your kitchen."

Betty's two small hands clasped each other mutely : her large eloquent eyes were raised to his in the sweetest glance that ever maiden gave.

" God bless you ! " she cried impulsively, and, turning, fled through the open door.

CHAPTER XIII

AT THE VLY MARKET

It was a bright sunny morning, but very cold, and snow lay packed hard and firm in the streets of New York, which, narrow as they were, afforded little opportunity for the sun's rays to penetrate with sufficient strength to warm the shivering pedestrians who were hurrying down Maiden Lane in the direction of the Vly Market. At the farthest end of the street were the shops, and one of these, "The Sign of the Cross Swords," stood within a stone's throw of the market itself. It was a small affair, with little grimy window-panes, where were displayed knives, scissors, and razors, with locks and keys of many odd sorts. At the door stood a half-grown boy, stamping his feet to keep warm, as he droned out in singsong fashion: "Walk in, gentlefolk, and have your razors ground ; we have all manner of kitchen furniture in cutlery within, also catgut and fiddle strings at most reasonable rates."

But these attractions did not appear to bring many customers inside the little shop, as the passers-by seemed chiefly eager to gain the Vly Market, where the stalls were crowded with purchasers who were getting the good things there displayed to indulge in keeping New Year's day with the proper spirit of festivity; and the shop-boy was about to slip inside for the comfort of warming his fingers and toes, when a tall, slender fellow in fisherman's dress accosted him.

" Hey, you there! Have you fish-hooks and nets within?"

" Aye, sir, in plenty. Will it please you to enter?" And the boy made room for the stranger to pass through the narrow doorway. The shop was apparently empty, except for a middle-aged man who rose from his seat on a high stool near the window, where he was busily engaged in polishing a pair of razors. As he came forward, the fisherman addressed him : —

" Good-day, friend. A frosty morning."

" But the wind will turn to east at sunset," said the other, with a quick glance from under his heavy eyebrows.

" A good wind, then, for the ' Sturdy Beggar,' " was the reply, as the fisherman clasped his hands behind his neck with a peculiar gesture.

" Then all's well," returned the shop-keeper, laying down his razors, and motion-ing his customer to come farther inside. " Whom do you seek here, sir ? "

" Mynheer Wilhelm Hoffmeister, known commonly as ' Billy the fiddler.' "

" He is off on duty since last Tuesday, but must be here to-night to play at a grand ball given at one of the Tory houses ; there must be news, for you are the third one who has asked for him since yesterday."

" News ? " said the fisherman eagerly ; " perhaps you have a billet for me ? "

" And what may you be called ? " asked the other cautiously.

" Jim Bates, from Breucklen Heights."

" Then you 're all right, sir ; why did n't you say so before ? " and the man, casting a swift glance to make sure that the boy at the door was not looking, pulled a scrap of dirty paper from his pocket, which was in-stantly seized and opened by the fisherman. As he read the few words it contained, the anxious lines on his face grew deeper.

" It is the only way," he muttered to him-self, as he tore the scrap into tiniest frag-

ments, " but I must know from Kitty the
hour." Then aloud, " Have you a bit of
paper, friend, on which I can write a message ? "

" Surely," said the shopkeeper ; " wait
here a moment until I fetch it," and he
went hurriedly through a small door at the
back of the shop, leaving the fisherman
standing near the window, from which he
could see the crowd outside. Suddenly the
man uttered an exclamation, and made a
dash for the door, nearly upsetting the boy
on the threshold.

" Tell your master I will return shortly,"
he said hurriedly, and disappeared in the
direction of the Vly Market.

It happened that Madam Cruger, thrifty
housewife though she was, had forgotten to
order an extra number of the large, flat
seedcakes, known as New Year Cakes (and
without which no gathering could be considered complete for New Year day, when
they were handed to all callers with the
accompanying glasses of mulled wine and
metheglin), and had therefore dispatched
her daughter, with a colored servant carrying
a capacious basket on his arm, to purchase
the dainty from the one stall in the Vly Mar-

ket where the aristocratic folk were wont
to deal. Truth to tell, Madam Cruger had
made matters somewhat uncomfortable for
her portly cook when she learned that the
cakes made by that functionary were too few
to meet her ideas of hospitality; and although
Kitty knew that it would require speed on
her part to go to the market and return in
time to dress and be ready to receive their
visitors in the drawing - room by twelve
o'clock, she preferred to pour oil on the
troubled waters and procure domestic peace
at the expense of a little personal fatigue.
Beside, it was not unpleasant to trip along
with the merry crowd, bent on enjoying
themselves, and Kitty knew that she would
meet many an acquaintance, out, like herself, on some belated errand for New Year
day.

But there was one occurrence for which
Kitty had not bargained, and that befell her
as she gained the market door. The fisherman, who had followed her as swiftly as he
dared without creating notice, passed close
at her elbow, then turned and met her face
to face. Kitty grew a little pale as he
touched his cap respectfully, but she stopped
in obedience to the glance which met hers.

"A Happy New Year to you, my good man," she said. "I fear that you and your brother craftsmen suffer this terribly cold winter. Stand aside out of the chilly wind which meets us through the market door and I will speak to you. Cato," to her servant, "go on to Frau Hansel's stall, and let her weigh out five pounds of seedcakes for my mother; I will join you there in a moment," and she turned back to the fisherman, knowing that in the crowd she was comparatively safe, provided her voice was not loud enough to attract attention.

"What is it?" she murmured, almost breathless from excitement, yet striving to maintain a quiet, even careless exterior. "I hoped you had fulfilled your dangerous errand and gone hence two days ago."

"I cannot leave until my mission is completed; we have almost certain news of an incursion by the British across the Kill von Kull, which will do much injury to the peaceful country folk of Elizabethtown and Newark. The man they call 'Billy the fiddler' will have a message for me to-night of the greatest importance, and he plays with others at the De Lancey ball; are you to be there, and at what hour?"

" I, Oliver?" said Kitty, and turned rosy red as the incautious word escaped her; "all New York is going at eight o'clock, but what has that to do with " —

" This," whispered Oliver Wolcott, pulling his hat further down over his eyes, and motioning Kitty to walk a few steps away from the door: " I must be there."

" You are mad!" and Kitty turned pale at the idea.

" Oh, no, I am coming as one Diedrich Gansevoort, from Albany. Do not fear for me; my disguise will be very perfect, and I go introduced by Abram Lansing, from whom I bring a letter to Madam De Lancey. They are old friends, though he is as stanch a Whig as she a Tory. I tell you, Kitty, 't is of vital importance that I ascertain the facts of this rumored raid upon the patriots, and I must risk all to gain it. Warn Betty, lest she give way to alarm: be brave and fear nothing."

" A Happy New Year, Mistress Kitty," said a gentleman who approached her, followed by his negro servant. " I shall do myself the honor to pay my respects to your mother a little later ; " and Mr. Van Brugh raised his three-cornered hat in courtly sa-

lute, staring hard at Kitty and the fisherman
as he passed them.

"We are noticed," said Oliver calmly;
"go on and do your errand."

"But I am so fearful for you," gasped
poor Kitty, whose usual composure seemed
to be deserting her. "You try me too far,
unless I may do something to aid your
escape, for a horrible sinking of my heart
seems to bode no good to you."

"Put no faith in omens," answered Oliver, with a smile. "I shall be off at daybreak. Farewell, Kitty, and have no fear;
I am well protected," and mingling in the
crowd, he passed out of the market door and
was gone.

With what courage she could summon,
Kitty sped on to Frau Hansel's stand. The
seedcakes had been weighed, decked with a
handful of Christmas greens, and placed in
the basket, and Kitty, after a few kind
words to the old Dutch market-woman, made
her way swiftly through the crowd and gained
the street.

"I must warn Betty," she thought as she
proceeded up Maiden Lane, and as she
came to Queen Street she paused. "Go
directly home," she said to her servant; "tell

my mother I have stopped to see Grandma Effingham and wish her a Happy New Year. I will be back in time to dress," and off she sped in the direction of Wall Street.

Betty, who like Kitty, had been spending her morning assisting in preparations for the New Year callers who would present themselves later in the day, was dusting the quaint Dresden Shepherdess who presided over a corner of the drawing-room mantel, when a sharp knock at the front door announced a visitor; and she fled out of the drawing-room only to encounter Kitty in the hall.

"A Happy New Year to you," said Kitty, in a tone of gayety which she was far from feeling. "I ran over to give greeting to grandma, and as I came my petticoat gave way; let me mount to your chamber and fasten it before I go to grandma's."

"Certainly," said Betty, and seizing hands both girls ran rapidly up the staircase. Inside the small chamber, Kitty closed the door, and set her back against it.

"The petticoat is fast enough, Betty, but I have something grave to say. Oliver is still in the city — he goes to the De Lanceys' to-night — I was to warn you."

" In what disguise?" asked Betty breathlessly.

" Indeed, I know not, except that he will represent Mynheer Diedrich Gansevoort, from Albany; oh, Betty, I am sore afraid."

"Nay, wherefore?" and Betty's eyes sparkled as her color rose. " We Wolcotts are not wont to fail, and I am now too accustomed to Oliver's hairbreadth escapes for fright."

" You were well alarmed at the servants' dance; oh, how rash he is!"

"We spare nothing in our country's cause," said Betty, with a proud little toss of her head; " but, Kitty, forgive me if I appear intrusive — I am puzzled to know how and where you and Oliver " —

"You should have known long ago," interrupted Kitty, blushing deeply, " but, somehow, I never could approach near enough to your heart to confess that Oliver and I are trothplighted though my mother's consent is lacking. We met in Albany — again at West Point, and oh, Betty, how I have longed to tell you. I have seen you look at me with eyes so like his; with such scornful glance when I laugh and jest with those hateful redcoats, such kindly smile when I showed you that I am at heart a patriot. Forgive me, dear, and let us do all we can to help Oliver to-night, for he is determined to be at the De Lanceys, as by going there he can obtain certain important information for the cause of freedom."

Betty threw her arms around Kitty; why did she feel as if the innocent words stabbed her? Had the "hateful redcoats" ceased to be hateful to her?

"Trothplighted," she whispered, with wide-open eyes of delight; "I hoped as much — how happy my father will be when Oliver"—

"Nay, nay," cried blushing Kitty, "you go too fast; think of madam, my mother, and her antipathy to the 'rebels,' as she calls them, quite forgetting that my aunt (where I made my home in Albany for three years) is one, as well as her naughty daughter. Good lack! my fortunes were told long ago had I but bowed to her wishes; and at the moment, Betty, — to let you into a profound secret, — the most desirable husband for me in her eyes is Captain Yorke."

"Indeed!" said Betty coldly, but Kitty was too engrossed in her own discourse to notice.

"Not that he has such an idea, mind you;

he loves to dance and jest with me, as a score of others do. But, Betty, your confidence in Oliver is well sustained so far, and it lightens my heart. Beside, there is no one here who would be apt to recognize him except you and me : though for the matter of that why Clarissa did not see and know his shadow at the servants' dance I have not yet ceased to marvel."

"You forget that she had no knowledge of his presence in New York, and Oliver has changed greatly since she saw him full three years ago."

"And now to grandma," said Kitty, releasing the latch of the door, which she had held carefully in her hand since entering the room, as a precaution against intruders ; "and fare you well, Betty, till we meet at the ball to-night."

All through that New Year day Betty's heart throbbed with excitement, as a steady stream of visitors passed in and out of the mansion, where Grandma Effingham and Clarissa bade welcome to old friends and young ones, to stately gentlemen in small clothes and powdered queues, with a fine selection of British officers, beginning with Sir Henry Clinton, who arrived in great

state and descended from his sleigh, with its
coal-black horses, accompanied by his aides,
for the English commander liked to concil-
iate the Tories of New York, and, as he
was then making secret preparations to accompany an expedition to South Carolina,
thought best to appear in public even more
than usual.

"Mistress Betty," said Geoffrey Yorke,
under cover of sipping a glass of port wine
which she had offered him, "I drink to your
very good health;" then softly, "I have not
seen you for a week; have you been quite
well since the Christmas party?"

"Is it so long?" — willfully; "Clarissa
said you called one day."

"Surely — to ask for you, and you never
came inside the room."

"Because I was busy, sir," replied Betty.
Then relenting as a swift remembrance
crossed her mind, "I was skating at the
Collect, where I went with Peter late in the
day."

"Will you dance with me to-night at the
ball — promise me all the dances you can
possibly spare?" and Geoffrey's voice took
its most tender tone as he fixed his eyes on
Betty's charming face.

" All my dances? Nay, two, possibly three, are as many as Clarissa would deem consistent with good manners," returned the maid, unable to forego the pleasure of teasing him; " indeed, I am bewildered even now remembering sundry engagements already made."

"The first dance, Betty," said Yorke pleadingly, as he saw the general taking leave, and prepared to accompany him. " Surely you will not deny me that grace?"

But Betty only gave him the tips of her fingers in reply as she swept a graceful courtesy. Was it the slight pressure of his hand which accompanied the farewell that made Geoffrey spring gayly into the sleigh and drive off with a half-boyish, half-triumphant smile?

CHAPTER XIV

THE DE LANCEY BALL

THE De Lancey mansion, then one of the most famous houses in New York, was on the Bloomingdale Road, and the drive out Bowery Lane ran through meadow - land and green trees in summer, but over hard-packed snow and ice in winter, for it was part of the highroad to Albany. So both Grandma Effingham and Clarissa ordered the fur muffs and hot-water bottles for the feet placed carefully in the sleigh, which Pompey brought to the door just as the night watch went down the street, crying in his slow, bell-like tones, " Eight o'clock, and all 's w-e-ll ! " Betty, standing muffled in long cloak and fur hood, on the steps of the house, said to herself, with a thrill of excitement, " All 's well ; please God I may say as much when midnight sounds to-night."

The sleigh was a large, roomy one, with back and front seats, and its big hood was

drawn up and extended like a roof over the
top, covering the heads of its occupants,
but open at the sides. Clarissa was seated
first, and well wrapped in the bearskin
robes which adorned the sleigh, and then
Betty tripped lightly down to have her little
feet bestowed in a capacious foot-muff, as
she carefully tucked her new gown around
her and sat beside Clarissa. Gulian, in
full evening dress, with small clothes, plum-
colored satin coat and cocked hat, took possession of the front seat. Pompey cracked
his whip, and the spirited horses were off
with a plunge and bound, as Peter, the irrepressible, shouted from the doorway, where
with grandma he had been an interested
spectator of proceedings, " A Happy New
Year to us all, and mind, Betty, you only
take the handsomest gallants for partners."

De Lancey Place had been the scene of
many festivities, and was famed far and
wide for its hospitality, but (it was whispered) this New Year ball was to excel all
others. The mansion stood in the centre
of beautiful meadow-land, with a back-
ground of dark pines, and these showed
forth finely against the snow which covered
the lawns and feathered the branches of the

tall oak-trees in front of the door. Lanterns gleamed here and there, up the drive and across the wide piazza; at the door were the colored servants, in livery imported direct from England, and from within came sounds of music. As Pompey swept his horses up to the step with an extra flourish of his whip, a group of British officers, who had just alighted from another sleigh, hastened to meet Clarissa and assist her descent.

"On my word, Clarissa," said Gulian, a few minutes later, as he offered her his hand to conduct her to the ballroom, "I never saw Betty look so lovely. Your pink brocade becomes her mightily, and her slender shape shows forth charmingly. Where did you procure those knots of rose-colored ribbon which adorn the waist? I do not remember them."

"That is my secret — and Betty's; she vowed the gown would not be complete without them, so I indulged the child, and I find her taste in dress perfect. Captain Sir John Faulkner seems greatly taken with her, does he not?"

"Aye, but let us hasten to find our hostess. They will be forming for the min-

uet directly, and you must dance it with
me, sweet wife, — unless you prefer another
partner."

Clarissa's reponse to this lover-like speech
was evidently satisfactory, for presently
Betty beheld her sister and Gulian take
places at the head of the room, next Madam
De Lancey, who opened her ball with Sir
Henry Clinton. Betty, since her arrival
in New York, had been trained and tutored
for the minuet by both Clarissa and Kitty,
and here was Captain Sir John Faulkner,
an elderly but gallant beau, supplicating
for the honor of her hand in the opening
dance.

"I am loth to decline," began Betty, a
little overpowered by the compliment, "but
I have already promised this dance."

"To me," said Geoffrey Yorke, at her
side, and looking up, Betty, for the first
time, saw her lover in all the bravery of
full uniform, powdered hair, and costly
laces. If he had been strikingly handsome
in the old homespun clothes in which he
first appeared before her on the shores
of Great Pond, he was ten times more so
now. Betty forgot that his coat was scarlet, that he represented an odious king and

all she had been taught to despise; she only
saw the gallant manly form and loving eyes
which met hers so frankly, and the hand
she gave him trembled as he led her out
upon the floor. For Betty did not know
— though the realization came to her later,
with bitter tears -- that all unconsciously
she had entered that fabled kingdom, the
knowledge of which makes life a mystery,
death a glory!

The music swelled on in slow and stately
measure: jewels flashed in the blaze of wax
candles, silken brocades rustled a soft ac-
companiment to the steps and courtesies
of their fair wearers, as Betty dreamed her
dream of happiness, only half aware that
she was dreaming. And when, at the close
of the minuet, Geoffrey led her to Clarissa,
there was no lack of gallants nor partners,
and Peter would have chuckled with delight
could he have seen that no one was so
eagerly sought for as the lovely, roguish
maid, who wore the knots of rose-colored
ribbon.

It was time for supper, and instruments
were being tuned into order for a grand
march, to be led by Madam De Lancey,
when Betty, standing near a large Indian

THE MINUET

screen, talking with Mr. Van Brugh, who
was a dear friend of her father's, became
aware of subdued voices at her elbow, on
the other side of the screen.

" I tell you I am right," said one of these
testily ; " I would stake my sword that he is
not what he seems. I saw him exchange
a bit of paper with yonder manikin fiddler,
who has been under suspicion for some
weeks, and cleverly they did it, too. It 's
not the first time, I 'll warrant, that Mynheer von Gam— "

" No, no, not Von at all ; you are safe to
be mistaken, Colonel Tarleton ; the gentleman is one Diedrich Gansevoort from the
Albany beverwyck. Madam De Lancey
herself made us acquainted : he is no spy."

Betty's heart sank. She murmured something in reply as Mr. Van Brugh paused.
This was the famous and cruel Colonel
Tarleton. If he had traced Oliver, then
all was lost. She strained her ears for
further information, smiling up at Mr. Van
Brugh as she waved her fan gently to and
fro.

" If you are so sure of it, why did he, an
apparent stranger, have aught to commu-
nicate to that fiddler yonder? Go quietly

through the crowd and watch the gentleman
as he appears at supper; I 'll have a word
with Yorke on the subject," and they moved
off in the direction of the ballroom.

" Will he, indeed?" thought Betty, as she
saw Geoffrey coming toward her from the
hall ; " not while I can hold him at my side,"
and with somewhat paler face, but with
calm demeanor she moved away, obedient
to Geoffrey's request that she should go to
supper.

Kitty Cruger's evening, unlike Betty's,
had been full of dangerous excitement.
Arriving at the ball with her mother, she
had been dancing with her usual spirit,
keeping, however, anxious watch for Oliver.
But she perceived no one whom she could
possibly imagine was he, even in disguise,
and therefore it was with almost a shock
of dismay that she found herself stopped,
as she was passing the supper-room door,
by her hostess, who " craved the favor of
presenting a gentleman just arrived from
Albany, who knew her family there." Kitty
dropped her most formal courtesy and raised
her eyes to the face of the stranger. Verily,
Oliver possessed positive genius for dis-
guises, and troubled as she was Kitty could

not restrain a smile as she recognized in the
rubicund countenance and somewhat portly
form of the gentleman bowing before her
an admirable caricature of no less a person
than her respected uncle, Cornelius Lansing, an antiquated Albany beau.

Yorke, with Betty, was just inside the
door as the pair entered, and as Kitty perceived them she paused for a moment to
say good-evening.

" Where have you been ? I was looking
for you. Permit me to present Mynheer
Gansevoort, of Albany. Mistress Betty
Wolcott and Captain Yorke. As for you,
sir," — to Yorke, with a playful tap of her
fan to engage his attention, — " you have
not yet claimed my hand for a dance. Pray,
what excuse can you devise for such neg-
lect ? "

Betty seized her opportunity. She must
warn Oliver at all hazards. " Have you
lately arrived ? " she said, fixing her eyes
on him ; then, in so low a whisper that it
barely reached him by motion of her lips,
" You are watched ; be careful ! "

" I am somewhat deaf," returned Oliver,
with great readiness, bending his ear toward
her. " By whom ? " — with equal caution.

"Colonel Tarleton. Escape as speedily as you can."

"Did you speak?" said Geoffrey, turning suddenly, to Betty's dismay, and casting a penetrating glance at Oliver, which he returned with the utmost calmness.

"This gentleman is somewhat deaf, I find," answered Betty. "It is a sad affliction, sir; has it troubled you long?"

"Some years. May I offer Captain Yorke a pinch of snuff?" and the pretended Mynheer Gansevoort produced a gold snuff-box from his waistcoat pocket, which he courteously extended to the English officer.

"You must excuse me; I have not yet acquired the habit," replied Geoffrey. "A glass of wine with you, sir, instead, if you will do me the honor."

"With great pleasure." And as they moved a step onward, Kitty passed first with Yorke, thereby giving Betty time to whisper to Oliver what she had overheard behind the screen.

"Your very good health, sir," said Geoffrey, as he took the glasses of port wine from a servant standing near the lavishly filled table; "and if you will not consider me intrusive, do you purpose stopping in New York?"

"That is as may be," replied the other. "I am not, however, returning to Albany immediately. Will you name a toast?"

"Aye," said Yorke quickly, raising his glass, with a searching look into Oliver's eyes, — "To your *safe* return to the Albany beverwyck; the climate of New York is somewhat unhealthy at present."

"Yorke," said a young officer, coming hastily up behind the group, "Colonel Tarleton desires speech with you for a moment; you will find him and Sir Henry by the screen in the ballroom."

"You heard?" whispered Betty, as Geoffrey left them; "Captain Yorke has recognized you — fly, fly, at once!"

"Is there another exit from this room, Kitty?" asked Oliver, finishing his glass of wine as he spoke, and handing the empty glass to the waiting servant.

"Only the window behind us," gasped Kitty; "quick! they are all too busy eating and drinking to notice if you slip through the curtains, and the balcony is but a few feet from the ground."

"Then I must run for it. Farewell," murmured Oliver, as the heavy damask curtains dropped back over his vanishing

figure. The two girls gazed into each
other's faces with dilated eyes and quivering lips. Would the alarm be speedily
given, and would they see him captured and
carried to certain death? For one breathless moment they listened, and then Kitty
turned sick and faint; her eyes closed as
Betty flung an arm around her waist.

"Some wine at once," she said aloud,
and two gentlemen sprang forward to assist
her to place Kitty in a chair. "She is
affected by the heat of the room; it will
pass in a moment," and she gave the reviv-
ing girl a good hard pinch, which made her
start in her chair. "Oh, Gulian, I am glad
you are here. Had you not better seek
Madam Cruger?"

"No, no," cried Kitty, struggling to rise,
and most heartily ashamed of herself for
her lack of self-control. "My mother is not
strong and must not be alarmed. I am
better; will you come into the hall with
me, Betty? It is cooler there."

"Of course, and you can rest awhile;
Gulian will bring us supper."

But supper and everything connected
with it was far from Betty's thoughts; all
she wished was a few words with Kitty

alone, which she knew Gulian's absence
would give her.

"Betty," said Kitty the instant he left
them, "you do not know half the danger.
If he has not the means of escape close at
hand — if the British officers arrest the
fiddler — Oliver is totally lost. Can you
see through yonder door if the man be there
still with the others?" Betty rose from
her chair and stepped inside the ballroom,
now nearly deserted, for the guests were
all at supper. She glanced eagerly toward
the upper end of the room; no, the manikin fiddler had disappeared. Then an idea
darted into her quick brain; inaction under
the circumstances was maddening; back she
darted to Kitty's side.

"Kitty, come with me instantly. We
will muffle ourselves in our cloaks and hoods
and steal forth for a moment. I'll find
Pompey and our sleigh, and if worst comes,
let Oliver fly in that fashion; Gulian's
horses are fleet enough to distance pursuers."

Without another word both girls flew
into the room near the front door where
they had left their wraps. Not a soul was
there: the servants had gone elsewhere,

knowing that their services would not be
required until the early morning hours, when
the ball broke up. It took but a moment
to pounce on their cloaks, and Betty also
seized a long dark wrap, which lay conven-
iently at her hand, thinking it might be use-
ful. Out into the hall they dashed swiftly
and silently, past the lanterns on the broad
piazza : and as luck had it, Pompey himself,
who had come up to witness the festivities
from the outside, popped up at the steps.

" What you 'se doin' hyar, little missy ? "
he began wonderingly, but Betty cut him
short.

" Fetch the sleigh at once, Pompey. Mistress Kitty is ill, and I want to take her
home."

Pompey, somewhat alarmed at the tone
and catching sight of Betty's white face
and burning eyes, vanished on the instant.
The girls drew into the shadow as far as
they were able, and holding their breath
peered into the darkness.

" What is that ? " whispered Kitty, as a
swift footstep crossed the piazza. " Oh, 't is
Yorke! Have a care, Betty, or we are
discovered," and she endeavored to drag
her farther back against the wall. As she

did so, the crouching figure of a man rose
up against the trunk of one of the oak-trees
on the lawn ; it was Oliver. His padded
coat cast off, they could dimly distinguish his
tall slender form. Some singular instinct
for which he could never account made
Yorke pause as he set his foot on the
threshold of the front door; he wheeled
just in time to see Betty's face, as one pale
ray from a distant lantern fell across it.

" Betty, what are you doing here?" he
cried, darting to her side. At that instant
a sound of voices broke on the stillness of
the night ; it came from behind the mansion
in the direction of the pine woods.

" Kitty is ill," faltered Betty. " I am
taking her home — do not, I pray you, detain me — oh, there is Pompey " — as the
welcome sound of sleigh-bells rang out on
the frosty air. " Geoffrey, Geoffrey, let me
go !"

Her tone of agonized supplication went to
Geoffrey's heart. Kitty flew down the steps
into the sleigh, unassisted, and Betty followed, her hand in Yorke's. There arose
a hoarse shout " The spy, the spy — he
has escaped by the road !" and as Betty
set her foot on the runner, a dark figure

vaulted over Kitty and buried itself in the
robes at the bottom of the sleigh.

"At last, sweetheart, I pay my debt,"
whispered Yorke in her ear, as he thrust
Betty safely into the seat. "Pompey, drive
for your life!" The startled negro needed
no second bidding, down came the whip-lash
on the horses' backs, and with a furious
plunge, a mad rear, they were off, a quarter
of a mile ahead before their pursuers turned
the corner of the mansion.

Oh, that wild race through the snow!
Even in after years, when long days of happiness had crowded out much of those stirring
times from Betty's mind, a shudder would
creep over her, and closing her eyes she
could see again the tall gaunt trees, the
frozen road, the snow that glittered so still
and cold in the cruel starlight, and hear
the distant shouts that she feared told of
pursuit. On they flew, Oliver giving occasional directions to the trembling and
excited Pompey. Now that he knew the
danger, the faithful negro would have died
sooner than fail to carry the fugitive into
comparative safety. On, through the Lispenard meadows, on, — until they struck
Broadway; no pursuers within sight, and

at Crown Street Oliver bade him turn in the direction of the river, and drive down until he reached the slip which lay at the foot of the street. All was still. Save an occasional belated pedestrian, nothing seemed stirring, and as they neared the dingy old tavern at the Sign of the Sturdy Beggar, Pompey pulled up his smoking, panting horses.

" Don't want to get too near dose lights," he said. pointing to the swinging lantern which adorned the hostelry : " darse n't let nobody see my young mistress ; Massa Gulian would flog Pompey for shuah if dis tale gets tole."

" You 're right, Pompey," answered Oliver, springing up and flinging the long dark cloak with which Betty had provided herself around his shoulders ; " take the ladies home slowly. Kitty, my beloved, farewell — farewell, Betty, brave little soul that you are ; I 'll tell my father how your quick wits came to my relief. Here I cross the river on the ice, and, God willing, reach the commander-in-chief with the tidings he desires by eight o'clock in the morning."

A sob from Kitty, a low " God guard you ! " from Betty, and Oliver vanished as

Pompey turned his horses and proceeded leisurely back to Broadway. The girls were literally too spent with emotion to do more than sink down breathless among the fur robes, and not one word did they exchange as they drove through Wall Street and finally drew up at the Verplancks' door. On the steps stood Gulian, a tall and silent figure, awaiting the truants.

"What does this mean?" he began sternly, as he lifted Kitty out. "Did the hue and cry for that wretched, miserable Whig spy frighten the horses? Clarissa is nearly distracted" —

"I will explain all to your satisfaction," interrupted Betty. "Meantime, listen, and be thankful;" and as she held up a warning hand, they heard through the stillness of the night the watchman's distant cry float down the frosty air: —

"Half past three o'clock — and all 's — well!"

CHAPTER XV

LOVE OR LOYALTY

"Do you mean to tell me that you, Clarissa's sister, had anything to do with the escape of a Whig spy?"

"Even so," said Betty calmly, though her face was pale and her brilliant eyes burning with excitement.

"Damnation!" retorted Gulian angrily. "Even your mistaken ideas of patriotism could hardly carry a well-behaved maiden so far."

"Gulian! how *dare* you!"

"What am I to conclude?" with a scornful wave of his hand; "your story is somewhat disjointed. Kitty is taken ill; you suddenly decide to carry her off in my sleigh without farewell of any kind to your hostess, without paying your sister or me the respect to ask permission. Then you state that a man — confound the beggar's impudence! — sprang into the sleigh, and you were foolish enough to fetch him out of the danger of pursuit, all because of loyalty to the cause of so-called freedom. I cannot understand — Stay! Captain Yorke was on the steps as I came out, hearing the shouts: did he witness this extraordinary occurrence?"

"I told you the fugitive had concealed himself in the bottom of the sleigh before I entered it," said Betty, terror seizing her lest a chance word should implicate Geoffrey in the matter. "Would you have me turn a helpless man loose among your Hessians? I have too vivid recollection of Nathan Hale's fate to contribute another victim to English mercy."

The taunt stung Verplanck, for, like many of the more liberal Tories, he had deeply deplored the tragic ending of the gallant Hale, although forced to regard it as one of the stern necessities of war. He bit his lip as he answered: —

"Thank you, Betty; I am glad Clarissa does not regard me as quite so bloodthirsty as you evidently deem me." Then, eying her keenly, as if struck by a sudden thought, "Did you know the man, or was it all pure patriotism?"

"Yes," returned Betty, filled with indignation at the sneer, and facing him with all her native courage; " yes, I know him well."

" Know him?" echoed the bewildered Gulian, " are you mad or am I dreaming?"

" Neither, I trust. The Whig spy, as you are pleased to call him, was my brother, Oliver Wolcott. Thank God that he has made good his escape, and congratulate yourself, Gulian, that you aided, even remotely, in it."

" Betty, Betty, if this be true, I trust Clarissa does not know."

" Never fear," with a choking sob; " I shall not tell her. She suffers enough, poor soul, with her husband upon one side and her people upon the other of this most cruel war."

" Betty, go to your chamber," said Gulian sternly. " I will myself escort Kitty to her own door, and impress upon her the necessity of keeping the matter a close secret. My mortification would be great were it known. Why, it might even endanger my friendship with Sir Henry Clinton."

Betty left the room, but her lip curled as she said to herself, " A Tory to the tips of his fingers; God forbid that I should ever feel what Clarissa must."

Very little sleep visited Betty that night
(or what remained of it) as she lay with
open eyes that strained into the growing
dawn, picturing to herself Oliver's flight
across the North River, and hoping fervently
that she had thrown the pursuit skillfully
off his track. When at last she fell into a
doze it was nearly seven o'clock in the morning, and Miranda, who softly entered the
room, bringing fresh water, halted at the
pillow, loth to waken her.

"Mistress Betty," she whispered. No
reply, but the sleeper turned uneasily, and
then opened her eyes. " I certainly do hate
to call you, but jes' look here ; what you say
for dat, little missy ? " and Miranda held up
a letter. " Dat was left wif me at daybreak by de young boy who came wif Sambo
— missy knows who I mean,"— rolling her
eyes fearfully around the room, — "and he
said tell you that Jim Bates, of Breucklen
Heights, had tole him to fetch it to you."

Betty seized the package ; it consisted of
a half-sheet of paper which inclosed a letter, doubled over and sealed with wax in the
fashion of the day.

" I am safely across the river," wrote
Oliver on the outer sheet, "and send this

to ease your mind and Kitty's. Moppet's
letter came to me inside one from my father
by private hand a few days since, on chance
of my being able to give it you. My service in the city is over, my object attained;
hereafter I shall be on duty with our troops.
God be with you till we meet again."

Betty broke the seal of her letter and
between sobs and laughter deciphered the
queer pot-hooks and printed letters with
which Miss Moppet had covered the pages.
Dear little Moppet : Betty could almost see
the frowns and puckered brow with which
the child had penned the words.

"My Betty dear," the letter ran, "we
miss you sorely, especially the Mare and me.
She whinnies when I seek the Stable, and I
was going to say I cry too, but never mind."
(This was partly erased, but Betty made it
out.) "It is so cold the Chickens are kept
in the kitchen at night lest they freeze. We
hope it may thaw soon, as we Desire to get
the maple syrup from the trees. Aunt
Euphemia is well. Miss Bidwell is still
knitting Socks for our poor soldiers, and I
made Half of one, but the Devil tempted
me with Bad temper and I threw it on the

Fire, for which I was well Punished. Pamela cries much; I do not see why she is so Silly. Sally Tracy is the only merry one, now you are away; she spends too much time, to my thinking, reading and walking with a young Gentleman who comes from Branford. I have not yet learned how to spell his Name, but you may Guess who I mean. When are you coming home, Betty? I want so to see your dear face. My Respects to Gulian and Clarissa, and Obedience to Grandma — I do not Recollect her whole Name. My Sampler is more perfectly Evil than ever, but I have completed the Alphabet and I danced on it, which Miss Bidwell said was Outrageous naughty, but my temper Felt calmed afterward. It has taken four Days to write this, farewell, from your lonesome little sister,

"FAITH WOLCOTT.

"Nota Bene. I send my Love to You know Who."

There were others of the Verplanck household who slept late that morning. Gulian's usually calm and somewhat phlegmatic temper had been moved to its depths by the startling and most unexpected revelation of

Oliver Wolcott's identity with the spy, whose escape Betty had aided and in which he was also indirectly implicated by the use of his horses and servant. Gulian's strict sense of justice told him that Betty was right in seizing the means at hand to rescue her brother, but that did not lessen his irritation at being used for anything which appertained to the Whig cause, for Gulian Verplanck was a Tory to the backbone. Educated in England, brought up to consider that the divine right of kings was a sacred principle, he carried his devotion to the Tories to such an extent that had he foreseen the conflict between King and Colonies it is safe to say he would never have wedded Clarissa Wolcott. His love for his wife was too great to permit him to regret his marriage, and he was too thorough a gentleman to annoy her by alluding to their political difference of opinion, except occasionally, when his temper got the better of him, which, to do him justice, was seldom. But Clarissa's very love for him rendered her too clear-sighted not to perceive the state of his mind, and the unspoken agitation which she suffered on this score had been partly the cause of her homesickness and longing

for her sister's companionship. He had
been both kind and considerate in sending
for Betty ; his conscience approved the ac-
tion ; and now to have this escapade as the
outcome was, to a man of his somewhat
stilted and over-ceremonious ideas, a blow of
the most annoying description.

When he sallied forth from his house
some two hours later than his wont, on his
way to the wharf, where his business was
located, he congratulated himself that he
had so far escaped questioning from his wife
on the occurrences of the night before.
When Betty left him, he had taken Kitty
home in the sleigh, and refrained from lec-
turing her except so far as insisting upon
her not mentioning the matter of Oliver's
escape to her mother. Exhausted as she
was, mirth-loving Kitty was moved to a
smile as she listened to Gulian's labored
sentences, in which he endeavored to con-
vince his listener and himself that what he
considered almost a crime against the King's
majesty — permitting the escape of a rebel
spy — was, so far as Betty was concerned, a
meritorious act. So Kitty promised, with
the utmost sincerity, that not one syllable
would she breathe of the matter to her

mother, or, in fact, to any human being, and
hugged herself mentally as she thought of
Gulian's horror if he only knew what a personal interest she had in that night's mad
race for freedom. Clarissa, sweet soul, had
lain down quietly, when told that their
horses had nearly run away, being badly
frightened by the hue and cry of an escap-
ing rebel; and uttering heartfelt thanksgiv-
ings that Pompey had brought the girls
home in safety, she went fast asleep and
remained so long after Gulian had risen,
breakfasted, and gone down Maiden Lane.

Business was somewhat dull that morning, and Gulian was conscious that each
time his office door opened he feared some
one would enter who had learned, he hardly
knew how, of his having been connected with
the hateful affair occupying his thoughts. It
was therefore with a genuine feeling of
relief that just as he was preparing to lock
up his books he heard the outer door open,
and a familiar voice inquire if he was
within.

"Pray come in at once, Yorke," he said,
throwing open the door of his private room
with alacrity, as he held out a hand of welcome to his visitor. "Did you rise early

this morning? I am ashamed to own how late I was, but the balls at De Lancey Place are promoters of sleep next day, I find."

"I can usually plead guilty to sleep," replied Yorke, throwing off his military cloak, and taking the chair which Gulian offered him, "but I had to be stirring early to-day, for Sir Henry had pressing affairs, and I was at headquarters before seven o'clock."

"Did you take horse in pursuit of the spy last night?" asked Gulian, with somewhat heightened color.

"Not I," answered Yorke carelessly; "the poor devil had luck on his side, or doubled marvelously well on his pursuers, for I am told that not a trace of him nor of his confederate, the little fiddler, did our men find. It's well for them, as Sir Henry was much enraged and their shrift would have been short, I fear, had they been captured."

"These rebels grow bolder than ever," said Gulian, uttering a secret thanksgiving which spoke better for his kindness of heart than his loyalty to King and Crown; "I marvel at their adroitness."

"So do we all; — but, Verplanck, I came on a different errand to-day than politics.

I came " — and Geoffrey hesitated, as a questioning look came on Gulian's face — " I came — I — In short, am I right in esteeming you for the present as brother and guardian to Mistress Betty Wolcott?"

" Aye ; in her father's absence, of course, I stand in that relation toward her. Well, what of Betty ?"

" Only this," and rising, Yorke bowed in courtly fashion : " I have the honor to ask your permission to pay my addresses to your sister, Mistress Betty."

" To Betty?" was Gulian's astonished and delighted response. " You surprise me. Your acquaintance is but recent, and, I think, somewhat formal?"

" Love is hardly a matter of time or formality," returned Yorke, with a smile, as a remembrance of his first meeting with Betty occurred to him, "and that I do truly and honestly love her you have my honorable assurance. Do you give me your permission to proceed in the matter?"

" With all my heart," said Gulian, this new aspect of things driving all unpleasantness connected with Betty from his head : " but her father's consent is, I fear me, quite a different matter."

"That is not for to-day," cried the lover, as he shook Gulian's hand with almost boyish delight, "and to-morrow may take care of itself if I can but gain Betty's ear."

"But my consent and Clarissa's can be but conditional," proceeded Gulian, his habitual caution returning to him. "I am not sure that I should be altogether justified — Nay," seeing Yorke's face cloud with keen disappointment, "I will myself lay the matter before Betty, and endeavor to ascertain if she may be well disposed toward you."

"Heaven forbid!" thought the impetuous lover. But he only said aloud, "Thank you, Verplanck, I am delighted to receive your sanction. How are you spending the afternoon?"

"I have business at Breucklen Heights, but I shall be at home this evening, when I will approach Betty in the matter, and tell my wife of the honor you do us. For I have not forgotten my many visits to your father, Lord Herbert, at Yorke Towers, and the kindness extended me while in England. Indeed, Yorke, for my personal share in the matter, I know of no alliance which could gratify me more."

This was unwonted warmth on Gulian's part, and Yorke, feeling it to be such, grasped his hand warmly at parting, as he flung himself in his saddle, and rode gayly up Maiden Lane.

But the "best laid plans o' mice and men" often meet with unsuspected hindrances, as both Gulian and Yorke were destined to discover. What special imp prompted Betty to sally forth for a walk after dinner, thereby missing a call from Yorke (who came thus early to prevent Gulian's intended interview), it would be vain to speculate; but when the maid returned, feeling more like her old happy self than she had done in weeks, the irony of fate prompted an encounter with her brother-in-law at the library door.

"I have somewhat to say to you, Betty," began Gulian, with an air of importance, which set Betty's nerves on edge at once. If there was one thing more than another that annoyed her it was Gulian's pompous manner. "Will you come inside before going upstairs? I will not detain you long."

Wondering what could have occurred to wipe out the displeasure with which he had dismissed her to bed the last time they met,

Betty followed him, and throwing off her
hood and cloak seated herself calmly as
Gulian entered and closed the door with the
solemnity he considered befitting the occasion.

" I had the unhappiness — the very great
unhappiness," he began, " to feel much displeased with you last night ; but upon thinking the whole matter over carefully, I am
convinced that in assisting your unfortunate
brother to escape you did your best under
the circumstances, and were justified in yield-
ing to a very natural and proper sisterly
impulse."

" Thank you," said Betty demurely, but
with a sparkle of fun in her liquid eyes
as she turned them upon Gulian, secretly
amused at this curiously characteristic apology.

" We will dismiss that event and endeavor to forget it ; I only wish to repeat my
injunction that I desire Clarissa should know
nothing of the matter." He paused, and
Betty made a movement of assent.

" How old are you, Betty ?" came the
next remark.

" I am turned sixteen," replied Betty,
somewhat surprised at the question.

"So I thought." Gulian paused again to give weight and dignity to the disclosure. "You are now of a marriageable age. I have this morning received a proposal for your hand."

"Indeed," said Betty calmly. "And who, pray, has done me that honor, in this city, where I am but a recent comer?"

"Precisely what I remarked; the acquaintance has been, perhaps, unduly short. But nevertheless a most honorable and distinguished gentleman intends to offer you, through me, his hand"—

"He had been wiser to present *me* with his heart," interrupted Betty, with a mischievous laugh. But mirth died on her lips as Gulian, frowning slightly, proceeded with his story in his own way.

"His hand, and I presume his heart; do not be flippant, Betty; it ill becomes you. This young gentleman will be called upon to fill a high position; he is the son of a man of title and"—

"Stay," said Betty coldly. "It is not necessary to rehearse his advantages. May I ask the name of this somewhat audacious gentleman?"

"Audacious?" ejaculated Gulian, falling

back a step to gaze full at the haughty face
uplifted toward him. "Surely you misun-
derstand me. Pending your father, General
Wolcott's consent, I trust you are able to
perceive the advantages of this match, for
Captain Geoffrey Yorke is a son of Lord
Herbert Yorke, and grandson of the Earl of
Hardwicke. It is an exceptionally good
offer, in my opinion, for any colonist, as in
this country, alas, we have no rank. Moreover, Betty, when the war ends it will be
wise to have some affiliation with the mother
country, and by so doing be in a position
to ask protection for your unhappy and misguided relatives who now bear arms against
the King."

Up rose Mistress Betty, her slender form
trembling with indignation, her eyes flashing, and her cheeks scarlet.

"I would to God," she cried passionately,
"that my father could hear you insult his
child, his country, and his cause. There is
no need for you to ask his consent to my
marriage with Captain Yorke, for here, this
moment, I promptly decline any alliance
which possesses the advantages you so feel-
ingly describe."

"Betty, Betty" — Gulian saw his mistake,

but it was too late; on rushed the torrent of her indignation.

"I wish you — and him — to understand that Betty Wolcott is heart and soul with her ' misguided relatives ' in rebellion against British rule; that nothing — no, nothing, would induce her to wed an enemy to her country."

"Nothing, Betty?" said a manly voice behind her, as Yorke himself crossed the threshold, where for the last few seconds he had been an angry listener to Gulian's blunders. "Surely you will grant me a moment to plead on my own behalf?"

"And wherefore?" cried Betty. "You sent your message by him," with a scornful wave of her hand toward Gulian's retreating figure; "through him, then, receive my reply."

"I will not," said Geoffrey firmly, as the door closed behind Verplanck. "Sweetheart, will you listen to me?"

"It is useless," murmured Betty, with a choking sob. "I was mad to even dream it might be possible. Gulian has made it all too plain to me."

"Nay, you must and shall hear me. I will not leave you until I tell you that I love you devotedly; ah, why should politics and war come between our hearts? Consider, Betty, I will do all a gentleman and a man of honor can to please you" —

"But you cannot desert your own people," she said despairingly. "I could not love you if you did, for, Geoffrey, it is but due you to confess in this hour of parting that you are very, very dear to me," and the last words just reached his eager ears as Betty sank, trembling, into a chair.

"Dearest," he cried, kissing the little hand which lay in his, "will you not bid me hope? Think, the tide may turn; we are both young, and who can predict the fortunes of war? I will not bind you, but to you I must myself be bound by the passionate love I bear you."

"Oh, Geoffrey, my beloved, it cannot be! I know what my dear and honored father would say. God guard you — farewell!"

He caught the dainty form in his arms, he held her next his heart and vowed that come what would he defied fate itself to separate her from him. "See," he cried, snatching the knot of rose-colored ribbon from his breast. "I will wear this token always as I have done since the day it dropped from your

gown on the grass. If it be twenty years,
I will yet come, with your father's consent,
to win you, and then, *then*, sweetheart, may
I claim my reward?"

"I cannot wed my country's foe," she
faltered. "Oh, Geoffrey, be merciful — let
me go." At that moment there came a vio-
lent knock upon the street door, a sound of
voices, and Pompey's slow step approaching
the library door.

"An express for Massa Captain brought
by Sir Henry's orderly," said the faithful
old negro, handing a sealed envelope to
Yorke, as he closed the door behind him.
Yorke tore it open; it fell from his hand.
For a moment he stood, tall, gallant, and
brave, before Betty; his eyes met hers in
long, lingering farewell.

"Sir Henry leads the expedition to South
Carolina to-night, Betty, and I go with him.
Nay, sweetheart, sweetheart, we shall meet
again in happier days."

She gave a little cry and flung herself into
his arms; she kissed him with all her warm
frank heart on her lips, and then she slipped
from his embrace and was gone as Yorke
dashed from the house, mounted his horse,
and galloped swiftly away.

CHAPTER XVI

MOPPET MAKES A DISCOVERY

IT was early autumn in Connecticut, and the maples had put on their most gorgeous robes of red and yellow. The weather had been mild for that region up to the middle of October, when a sudden light frost had flung its triumphant banner over hill and dale with a glow and glory seen to its greatest perfection in New England. The morning air was somewhat fresh, and Miss Bidwell, hearing Moppet's feet flying along the hall, opened the door of the sitting-room and called the child.

"You will need your tippet if you are going beyond the orchard, and I think perhaps your hood."

"Hood!" echoed Miss Moppet disdainfully, shaking her yellow curls over her shoulders until they danced almost of themselves; "I do not need to be muffled up as if I were a little girl, Miss Bidwell. You forget I was twelve years old yesterday," and she waltzed around the room, spreading her short skirt in a courtesy, to Miss Bidwell's admiring gaze.

" Indeed, I am likely to recollect when I myself arranged the twelve candles in your birthday cake."

" To be sure ! " cried Moppet, with swift repentance, "and such an excellent, rich cake as it was, too. Do you think " — insinuatingly — " that I might have a slice, a very tiny slice, before I go forth with Betty to gather nuts in the Tracys' woods ? "

" No," replied Miss Bidwell, laughing, " you will assuredly be ill if you touch one morsel before dinner. Run along, Miss Moppet, I see your sister waiting for you at the gate," and Moppet, with a jump and a skip, flew off through the side door and down the path, at the end of which stood Betty.

It was a very lovely Betty over whom the October sunshine played that morning, but to a keenly observant eye a different Betty from her who had danced at the De Lancey ball, now nearly three years past. This Betty had grown slightly taller, and there was an air of quiet dignity about her which suggested Pamela. But the beautiful merry eyes had deepened in expression, and it was, if anything, a still more attractive face than of old, although the fair unconsciousness of childhood had departed ; and if mischief still lurked in the dimpled cheeks, that was because Betty's heart could never grow old ; no matter what life might hold for her of joy or sorrow, she would always be to a certain extent a child. And well for her that it was so ; do we not all know a few rare natures whose fascination dwells in this very quality ?

The years had gone swiftly for Betty. Shortly after her parting with Yorke an opportunity had occurred for her return to Litchfield, and although Clarissa lamented her departure Betty was eager to fly home. Gulian had done his best to smooth over his ill-judged and ill-tempered effort to arrange her matrimonial affairs, and one of Betty's minor annoyances was her sister's evident disappointment at Yorke's rejection. Only once had she forgotten herself and flashed out upon Clarissa, peremptorily forbidding further discussion, and Clarissa had been positively aghast at the impetuous little creature who confronted her with flashing eyes and quivering lips, and had speedily

warned Gulian never to broach the subject
to Betty again. Peter was Betty's closest
friend in those stormy days. The urchin
had a shrewd perception of how matters
stood, and many a time had Betty hugged
him for very gratitude when he made a
diversion and carried her off to some boyish
haunt in the city or to the Collect, thereby
giving her opportunity to regain the self-
control and spirit necessary to appear as
usual. For Betty was formed of gallant
stuff. No matter if her heart ached to
bursting for sight of Geoffrey, if her ears
longed, oh, so madly, for the sound of his
voice; she could suffer, aye, deeply and
long, but she could also be brave and hide
even the appearance of a wound. That
Gulian, and even Clarissa, considered her a
heartless coquette troubled her not at all,
and so Betty danced and laughed on to the
end of her sojourn in New York.

It had always been a source of thankful-
ness to her that she had been able to go
home before Geoffrey's return from the
expedition to South Carolina, for she sometimes doubted her own ability to withstand
his personal appeal if again exerted. That
he had returned and then, shortly after, gone

upon another detail, she had heard incidentally from Oliver during one of her brother's flying visits to Litchfield on his way to New London with dispatches. Oliver had been greatly touched by Yorke's conduct in the matter of his escape, but if he suspected that Betty's lovely face had anything to do with the British officer's kindly blindness, he was too clever to hint as much, for which forbearance Betty thanked him in the depths of her heart. The only way in which he showed his suspicion was in the occasional bits of news concerning Yorke with which he favored her. At the battle of Cowpens Yorke had been wounded and taken prisoner, and it fell to Oliver Wolcott to arrange for his exchange. Then, for the first time, were Oliver's surmises changed to certainties, for one night when he had been attending the prisoner, whose wound was nearly healed, Yorke broke silence and in the frankest, most manly fashion demanded news of his little sweetheart, and told Oliver of his hopes and fears. Nothing could have appealed so directly to the brother as Yorke's avowal that Betty had refused him because of the coat he wore, and his eyes filled as he said, boyishly enough, " Egad, Yorke, she has all the Wolcott pluck and patriotism; though were this vexed question of independence settled, I wish with all my heart that you may yet conquer this unwilling maid whom I call sister."

Yorke smiled, but he did not consider it necessary to add that Betty had once let compassion and gratitude get the better of her loyalty in the matter of a prisoner, to Oliver's own discomfiture.

There had been some changes in the Wolcott home : Pamela had gone forth from the mansion a bride, after Cornwallis had surrendered at Yorktown, and Josiah Huntington had worn a major's uniform on his wedding-day. Betty had scarcely recovered from that break in the home circle when Sally Tracy, with many blushes and much laughter, confessed that she, too, was about to follow Pamela's example, and that a certain Mr. James Gould, the gentleman from Branford, of whom Moppet had been so suspicious, was the lucky individual upon whom she intended to bestow her hand. Verily, with all these wedding-bells sounding, Betty began to feel that she was likely to be left alone, but she only laughed gayly when twitted with her fancy for maidenhood, and danced as merrily at Sally's wedding as if her heart had lain light in her bosom instead of aching bitterly for one whom she began to fear she should never see more.

Little did Betty guess that bright October morning, when she and Moppet went forth bent on a nutting excursion, that a courier was even now speeding on his way whose coming would change the tide of her whole existence. And when, as noon struck, Oliver Wolcott dismounted at the door of his home and, walking straight to his father's study, delivered a packet from General Wolcott to Miss Euphemia, his next move was a descent upon Miss Bidwell's parlor and a hasty demand for Betty. So when Moppet and Betty appeared, rosy with success and a fair-sized bag of nuts as the result of their joint labors, they found the household in a state of suppressed excitement, and lo! the cause was Oliver's approaching marriage.

"You see," explained Oliver, when he finally got Betty to himself for a walk in the orchard after dinner, "now that the treaty has been signed in Paris, the British will soon evacuate New York, and when our army enters, there will be grand doings to celebrate the event, and my father must ride at the head of the Connecticut troops on that day. I, too, Betty, God willing, shall be with the Rangers, and thinking the date will be about a month hence, Kitty and Madam Cruger have set our wedding-day as the 25th of November. I gave you Kitty's letter " —

" Yes, and a dear, kind letter it is. She bids me for her bridesmaid, Oliver, and says that Moppet and Peter will hold her train, after the new English fashion (which no doubt is her mother's suggestion, for I think Kitty does not much affect fancies which come across the water), and, oh, Oliver, I do indeed wish you joy," and Betty's eyes brimmed full of tears as she gave him her hand.

" I know you love Kitty," said Oliver, kissing her cheek, " and we can afford to forgive a wedding after the English mode, as, if I gain my Kitty, I care but little how she comes."

" Betty, Betty," called Moppet's voice from the upper path, " do come in if you and Oliver have finished your chat, for Miss Bidwell desires your opinion on some weighty matter connected with our journey to New York."

" I will come," answered Betty; then turning back with as careless an air as she could summon, " Do you happen to have heard aught of your quondam prisoner, Captain Yorke ? "

" Yorke ! " replied Oliver, avoiding her eye as he stooped to throw a stick from the path, — " Yorke ! oh, aye, I did hear that he was invalided and went home several months ago. I fancy it was not so much his health (for he looked strong enough to my thinking the last time I met him) but more his disgust with the turn things were taking ; for you know, Betty, since the surrender at Yorktown the British have been more insolent and overbearing than ever, and Yorke is too much a gentleman, no matter what his political color, to be dragged into quarrels which I hear are incessant in the city, and the cause of many duels."

" Duels ! " cried Betty, as the color left her cheeks; " oh, I hope he — that is — I hope nobody whom I know has been engaged in one."

" Not I," returned Oliver, with a mischievous glance. " So you might even be sorry for a foe, eh, Betty ? " But Betty went flying up the path and did not deign to reply.

Miss Moppet, childlike, was perfectly overjoyed at the prospect of a wedding in which she was to play a part, and flew from her aunt to Miss Bidwell and Betty, then back to her aunt again in a twitter of excitement at the combination of a journey and festivity as well. General Wolcott's letter to his sister was full of important news. As the seat of Congress was Annapolis, General Wolcott, who was a member of that body, had decided to close the manor house for the winter and take a house in New York for his family, and he sent minute and particular directions for leaving all home affairs in the hands of Miss Bidwell and Reuben until their return to Litchfield in the spring. Oliver's intended marriage had hastened this decision, and there would be barely time to settle matters and reach New York in season for the wedding. They were to stop with Clarissa, who had written most pleading letters, and after that visit would take possession of their new quarters.

Most of the afternoon was spent in plans for their journey, with Oliver as escort, and many a sigh rose almost to Betty's lips as these recalled that other journey when her heart had been as light as Moppet's was now.

But she put all thought aside with a resolute heart, and finally receiving directions from Miss Euphemia in regard to a chest of winter clothing packed safely away in the garret, she concluded to give Moppet's restless hands some occupation, and bade the child accompany her upstairs.

The old garret looked familiar enough. Even the wooden stools which had served as seats for her and Sally Tracy in the old childish days stood in the same corner under the dormer window, through which the sun was even now pouring its setting rays. The chest was unlocked, and presently a goodly pile of clothing lay upon the floor ready to be carried below.

"Let me have my worsted jacket, and my flannel wrapper (indeed, I do believe they are too small for me; can I find others in New York, Betty?), and this pretty hood of Pamela's. Betty, Betty, do you think Miss Bidwell could cut this one smaller for me? May I just run down and ask? I will return at once."

"Yes," said Betty, intent upon counting a heap of stockings; "please fetch me a pair of scissors when you come up again."

Off flew Moppet, marking her progress

down the garret stairs by various exclamations as she dropped the jacket and tripped on the wrapper, but finally reached the bottom in safety. Betty went on overlooking the chest; there were many articles to select from, and a red skirt of Moppet's which did not appear to be forthcoming. She ran her hand down to the very bottom of the chest, and feeling some garment made of smooth cloth with a gleam of red in it, dragged it forth and held it up to the light. As she did so, her hand struck something hard and round.

" What have I found?" thought Betty, but the next moment she saw that what she held was an officer's dark blue riding-cape fastened with brass buttons, on each of which was engraved a crown, and the cape was lined with British scarlet.

" What have you got there?" said Moppet's voice, as she appeared at her side. " Why, 't is Captain Yorke's cape that he muffled me in the day I fell into Great Pond — Oh, Betty, Betty, what is amiss?"

Down on her knees fell Betty. She buried her face in the cape's folds, and tears rolled down her cheeks as she tried to say, " It is nothing, nothing, I am tired — I am

—Oh, Geoffrey, Geoffrey, I think my heart
is breaking."

Miss Moppet opened her eyes to their
widest; then slowly and deliberately she
grasped the situation in "high Roman fashion."

"Betty Wolcott, do I live to see you weep
over a scarlet coat!"

No answer; indeed, Betty scarcely heard
the words. The flood-gates were let loose
and the agony of days and months must
have its way.

"Betty!" this time the voice of reprov-
ing patriotism quavered somewhat. "I do
believe you are worse than Pamela." But
Betty sobbed on, — sobs that fairly racked
her slender body.

"Well, I don't care what anybody says,"
— and Moppet flung the Whig cause to the
wind as she cast herself down beside Betty,
—"he's dear and handsome and brave;
whether he be British or Yankee, I love him,
and *so do you*, naughty, naughty Betty!"

And with her head on Miss Moppet's
sympathizing shoulder, and Miss Moppet's
loving arms clasped around her neck, Betty
Wolcott whispered her confession and was
comforted.

CHAPTER XVII

A KNOT OF ROSE-COLORED RIBBON

THE sun rose bright and clear over the Bay of New York. It had been a somewhat gray dawn, but the fog and mist had gradually rolled away, and the day bid fair to be one of those which Indian summer occasionally gives in our northern climate. All around Fort George and the Battery the British troops were making ready for departure; the ships for their transportation to England lay out in the bay, for this was the 25th of November in the year of our Lord 1783.

The streets in the upper part of the city were filled with a different kind of crowd, but one equally eager to be off and away. Many of the Tories and sympathizers with the Crown had found New York a most unpleasant dwelling-place since the signing of the treaty in which "The United States of America" were proclaimed to the world an independent Power, and Sir Guy Carleton,

the British commander, had more trouble
in providing transportation for this army of
discontented refugees than for his own soldiers. However, the day was fixed, the
ships ready to weigh anchor, and the Army
of Occupation about to bid adieu to American shores forever.

" Peter," said Miss Moppet, as she danced
merrily out of the breakfast-room, " you are
sure, quite sure that the grand procession,
with General Washington at its head, will
come past this door ? Because we are all
cordially bidden to Mistress Kitty's and perhaps Betty may prefer to go there."

" But it will be a far better sight here,"
returned Peter; " it is sure to pass our door,
for I heard Oliver tell Aunt Clarissa so last
night just as he was going out."

" Oliver has overmuch on his mind to-day,"
remarked Moppet shrewdly ; " to ride with
his troop in the morning and be married at
evening is quite enough to make him forget
the route of a procession. Do you think we
might go out on the doorstep and see if
there be any sign of its approach ? "

" Why not ? It will be royal fun to see
the British soldiers come down from the
Government House, and hear the hoots and

howls the Broadway and Vly boys are bound
to give them. For once all the boys of the
city are of one mind — except the Tory boys,
and they don't count for much hereafter."

" I wouldn't jeer at a fallen foe if I were
you, Peter," said Moppet severely, as she
took up a position on the stoop, and leaned
her elbows on the iron railing; "my father
says that is not manly, and besides I do suppose there may be some decent Britishers."

" I never knew but one," retorted Peter
stoutly. " What knowledge have you of
them, I'd like to know ? "

" Not much," evasively. " Who was the
one you mention ? "

" My ! but he was a prime skater ; how he
and Betty used to fly over Collect Pond that
winter. Do you skate up in Litchfield,
Moppet ? "

" Yes, of course ; that's where Betty
learned with Oliver."

" Oh, aye, I remember ; when she cut a
face on the ice the day she raced with Captain Yorke she told me her brother had
taught her."

At this moment there was sound of a distant bugle ; both children ran down to the
foot of the steps and gazed eagerly up the

street. But it was a false alarm, and after
a few moments spent in fruitless watching
they returned to their post of observation on
the stoop.

" Peter," began Moppet presently, with
true feminine persistency, " what were you
saying about a British officer who knew
Betty ? "

" Captain Yorke ? He was aide to Sir
Henry Clinton."

" Was he ? Will he go off to-day with all
the other redcoats ? "

" He sailed away to England some months
ago, — I recollect he came to bid good-by
to Clarissa, — but do you know, Moppet,"
lowering his voice, with a glance over his
shoulder to be certain that he was not overheard, " I think I saw him two days ago."

" In New York ? " said Moppet, with a
start. " Why you said he 'd gone to England."

" But he could come back, surely. Moppet, *I* think he was proper fond of Betty."

" Peter Provoost, do you fancy that my
sister would smile on a scarlet coat ? You
ought to be ashamed of yourself," and Moppet looked the picture of virtuous indignation.

" Well, I've seen her do it," retorted
Peter, not in the least abashed, " and what's
more I heard him call her ' sweetheart '
once."

" Oh, Peter ! " Moppet's curiosity very
nearly got the better of her discretion ; but
she halted in time, and bit her tongue to
keep it silent.

" And if you won't tell — promise ? " —
Moppet nodded — " not a word, mind, even
to Betty — where do you think I saw Captain
Yorke the other day ? You'll never guess ;
— it was at Fraunces's Tavern on Broad
Street, and he was in earnest conversation
with General Wolcott."

" With my father ? " This time Moppet's astonishment was real, and Peter
chuckled at his success in news-telling.

" Children," called a voice from the hall,
" where are you? Do you want to come
with me on an errand for Clarissa near Bowling Green, which must be done before the
streets are full of the troops ? "

" Surely," cried both voices, as Peter
dashed in one direction after his cocked hat,
and Miss Moppet flew in another for the
blue hood. Betty waited until the pair returned, laughing and panting, and then tak-

ing a hand of each she proceeded up Wall
Street to Broadway, and down that thor-
oughfare toward Bowling Green. Before
they had quite reached their destination the
sound of bugle and trumpet made them turn
about, and Peter suggested that they should
mount a convenient pair of steps in front of
a large white house, which had apparently
been closed by its owners, for a number
of bystanders were already posted there.
They were just in time, for around the corner of William Street came a group of officers on horseback, their scarlet uniforms
glittering in the sun. It was Sir Guy Carleton and his staff, on their way to the Battery, where they would take boats and be
rowed over to a man-of-war which awaited
them in the bay. A murmur, then louder
sounds of disapprobation, started up from
the street.

"There they go!" cried a voice, "and
good riddance to Hessians and Tories."

Betty's cheeks flushed. Oh, those hateful scarlet coats, symbols of what had caused
her so much misery. And yet — with another and deeper wave of color — it was
Geoffrey's uniform and these were his brother officers, going where they would see

him ; oh, why, why, was fate so unkind, and life so hard! Another moment and they were out of sight, but keen-eyed Moppet caught a glimpse of Betty's downcast face and said to herself, "Oh, I dare not tell her ; I wish I did."

Out on Bowery Lane and away up in Harlem, over King's Bridge, with measured step and triumphant hearts the Continentals were entering the city. What a procession was that, with General Washington and Governor Clinton at its head, and how all loyal New York spread its banners to the wind and shouted loud and long to welcome it! There were the picked men of the army, the heroes of an hundred fights, the men of Massachusetts who had been at Lexington and Bunker Hill ; General Knox in command, and General Wolcott with his Connecticut Rangers, while Oliver rode proudly at the head of his company. It was a slow march, down the Bowery and through Chatham and Queen streets to Wall, thence up to Broadway, where the column halted.

It would be vain to describe Betty's emotion as from the windows of the Verplanck mansion she watched the troops and the civil concourse, and realized that at last, after long years of heroic endurance, of gallant fighting, of many privations, the freedom of the Colonies was an accomplished fact. Miss Moppet and Peter flew from one window to another and cheered and shouted to their hearts' content. Even Grandma Effingham and Clarissa waved their handkerchiefs, while Gulian, on the doorstep, raised his cocked hat in courtly salute to General Washington. Gulian was beginning to learn that perhaps one might find something to be proud of in America, even if we were lacking in the rank and titles he so admired.

Oliver's wedding, which was set for six o'clock, to allow the commander-in-chief to be present before the banquet at Fraunces's Tavern, was to be on as grand a scale as Madam Cruger's ideas could make it; for having consented to her daughter's marriage, that stately dame proposed to yield in her most gracious fashion. It took some time to dress Miss Moppet in the silken petticoat and puffed skirt, the tiny mobcap and white ribbons, which Kitty had considered proper for the occasion, and Betty found she must hasten her own toilet, or be late herself. Moppet followed her up to the old room where Betty had spent so many hours of varied experience, and assisted to spread out once again the flowered brocade, which had not seen the light of day since the De Lancey ball.

"Here are your slippers, Betty; how nicely they fit your foot."

"Yes," said Betty, her thoughts far across the sea, as she slipped on one of them.

"I hope these are wedlock shoes," quoth Moppet, with a queer, mischievous glance, as she tied the slipper strings around the slender ankle. But Betty did not heed her; she was busy undoing the knots of rose-colored ribbon on the waist, which she had once placed there with such coquettish pride.

"What are you about?" cried Moppet, seizing her sister's hand as she was in the act of snipping off one with the scissors. "Oh, Betty, the gown will not be half so pretty without them."

"Nay, child, rose-colored ribbons are not for me to-day; I am grown too old and sad," said Betty softly, looking with tender eyes into Moppet's face.

"Did ever I hear such fal-lal nonsense,"

and Moppet's foot came down in a genuine
hot-tempered stamp which made Betty start.
" Betty, Betty, I will not have it — pray put
them back this moment; " then in the coaxing voice which she knew always carried her
point, " What would Oliver and Kitty say
if you were not as gay as possible to grace
their wedding ? Oh, fie, Betty dear ! "

As usual Moppet had her way, and when
the pair alighted at the Cruger door Betty's
knots of rose-color were in their accustomed
place.

Within the mansion all was light and gay.
Weddings in those times were conducted
with even more pomp and ceremony than in
our day, and the entertainments, though not
upon the present scale, were fully as lavish.
Wax candles shone at every possible point,
and lit up the broad reception-hall, the polished floors and high ceilings, while mirrors
on mantels and walls reflected back many
times the stately figures which passed and
repassed before them. And then there came
a pause, when voices were hushed, and down
the oak staircase came Kitty, led by Gulian
Verplanck (her nearest male relative), wearing a white satin petticoat (though somewhat scanty to our ideas in width and

"I HOPE THESE ARE WEDLOCK SHOES"

length), and over it a train of silver brocade, stiff and rustling, while a long scarf of Mechlin lace covered her pretty dark head and hung in soft folds down her back. The high-heeled slippers, the long lace mitts, with their white bows at the elbow, completed her toilet. She stood before the assembled company a fair young bride of the olden days, and behind her came Miss Moppet and Peter Provoost, holding her silver train with the tips of their fingers. Oliver, in full Continental uniform, his cocked hat under his arm, awaited her at the end of the great drawing-room, and with somewhat shortened service, the rector of old St. Paul's said the words which made the pair man and wife.

Betty was standing near the mantel, laughing and chatting gayly with several of her former New York gallants, when she beheld her father advancing toward her on the arm of a gentleman. Surely she knew that tall, elegant figure, that erect, graceful carriage? But the scarlet uniform which was so familiar was absent ; this was the satin coat, smallclothes, and powdered hair of a civilian. Betty's head swam, her brilliant color came and went, as her father said quietly : —

"My daughter, an old acquaintance desires that I should recall him to your recollection : I trust it is not necessary for me to present to your favor my friend, Mr. Geoffrey Yorke."

Betty's knees shook as she executed her most elaborate courtesy, and as if in a dream she heard General Wolcott say to Yorke, with a somewhat quizzical smile, " Perhaps you will kindly take Betty to the library, where I will myself join you later after escorting General Washington to the banquet."

Betty never knew how she crossed that room ; every effort of her mind was concentrated in the thought that she must not betray herself. What did all this mean? Such a blaze of sunshine had fallen upon her that she did not dare look at it ; she only realized that her hand was in Geoffrey's until they reached the quiet and deserted library, and then he was at her feet.

" Sweetheart, sweetheart," he said, " you will not refuse to hear me now? I have resigned the army, I have left England forever (unless you yourself will some day accompany me there to meet my people), I have thrown in my fortunes with the United States, and doubt not I will prove as faithful a servant to your Commonwealth as I ever was to King George," and kissing her hand, he laid in it the faded knot of rose-colored ribbon.

"But, Geoffrey," she faltered, "my father" —

"Did not General Wolcott himself bid me fetch you here? Ah, Betty, the conditions are all fulfilled, and you are still unwilling."

She looked at him for a moment in silence, and then her most mischievous smile dawned in Betty's eyes as she hid Geoffrey's little knot of ribbon in her gown.

"My heart, but not my will, consents," she said. "Dare you take such a naughty, perverse rebel in hand for life?"

"I dare all for love of Betty Wolcott," cried the triumphant lover, while from the door a small person in mobcap surveyed the pair with very round and most enraptured eyes.

"It's just like a fairy tale," quoth Miss Moppet, "and I'm in it!"

www.ingramcontent.com/pod-product-compliance
Lightning Source LLC
Chambersburg PA
CBHW030344270326
41926CB00009B/956